# The Customer
# Service
# Training
# Tool Kit

**Also by Val and Jeff Gee**

*Super Service: Seven Keys to Delivering Great Customer Service*
This brief companion volume to *The Customer Service Training Tool Kit* is written specifically for front-line customer service providers.

# The Customer Service Training Tool Kit

60 Activities for Delivering
Super Service to Customers

**Val Gee**

**Jeff Gee**

Boston, Massachusetts    Burr Ridge, Illinois
Dubuque, Iowa    Madison, Wisconsin    New York, New York
San Francisco, California    St. Louis, Missouri

**Library of Congress Cataloging-in-Publication Data**

Gee, Val.
    The customer service training tool kit : 60 activities for delivering super service to customers / Val and Jeff Gee.
      p.    cm.
    ISBN 0-07-913773-3
    1. Customer services—United States.   2. Employees—Training of—United States.   I. Gee, Jeff.  II. Title.
HF5415.5 .G443     2000
658.8'12—dc21                                          99-047597

## *McGraw-Hill*

*A Division of The McGraw·Hill Companies*

2 3 4 5 6 7 8 9 0   BKM/BKM   9 0 9 8 7 6 5 4 3 2 1 0 9

ISBN 0-07-913773-3

*The sponsoring editor for this book was Richard Narramore, the editing supervisor was Fred Dahl, and the production supervisor was Elizabeth Strange. It was typeset in New Baskerville by Inkwell Publishing Services.*

*Printed and bound by Bookmart Press.*

# Contents

# Find the Activity That's Just Right for Your Audience!

| Activity no. and name | Team Building | Perception | Attitude | Motivation | Listening | Problem Solving | Communication | Understanding Needs | Selling | Self-Assessment |
|---|---|---|---|---|---|---|---|---|---|---|
| 1. Why Should I Give Super Service? | * | * | * | * | * | * | * | * | * | * |
| 2. Moments of Truth | * | * | * | * | * | * | * | * | * | * |
| 3. How to Revitalize My Energy | | * | * | * | | | | | | * |
| 4. Super Service Self-Assessment | * | * | | | | * | | | | * |
| 5. How Do I Feel About My Customers? | | * | * | * | | | | | | * |
| 6. Identifying External and Internal Customers | * | | * | | | * | | * | | * |
| 7. Serving Your Best When Feeling Your Worst | | | | * | | * | | * | | * |
| 8. How to Show a Desire to Serve | | | * | | | * | | | * | * |
| 9. Who Teaches Me Super Service? | | * | | * | * | | * | | | * |
| 10. Affirmations | | | * | | | | * | * | | * |
| 11. How to Take Responsibility | * | * | * | * | * | | * | * | | * |
| 12. Clear a Space in My Life | | * | * | | | * | | * | | * |
| 13. How to Walk My Talk | | * | * | | * | * | * | * | * | * |
| 14. The Right Attitude | | | * | | * | * | * | * | | * |
| 15. Preparing for a Customer Interaction | * | * | | | * | * | * | * | * | * |
| 16. Maintaining a Positive Frame of Mind | | | * | * | | * | * | * | * | * |
| 17. Understand the Customer's Needs | * | | | | * | * | * | * | * | * |
| 18. How to Listen with an Open Mind | | | | | * | * | * | * | * | * |
| 19. Visualization Technique: Talking with Customers | * | * | | * | | * | | | | * |
| 20. How to Use Open and Closed Questions | | | * | | * | * | * | * | * | * |
| 21. Verify and Clarify Needs | | | | | * | | * | * | * | * |
| 22. Barriers That Inhibit Problem Solving | * | | * | | * | * | * | * | | * |
| 23. Honesty as a Tool | * | * | | | * | * | * | | * | * |
| 24. Work Together | * | | * | * | * | * | * | * | * | * |
| 25. How to Give Information | | | | | * | * | * | * | * | * |
| 26. Product Profile from a Customer Perspective | * | | * | | * | | * | * | * | * |
| 27. How to Give Unwelcome Information | * | * | * | | * | * | * | * | * | * |
| 28. Acknowledge the Customer's Feelings | | * | | | * | | * | * | | * |
| 29. When to Call In the Manager | * | | * | | * | | * | * | * | |
| 30. Reach Agreement | * | | * | | | | * | * | * | * |

| Activity no. and name | Team Building | Perception | Attitude | Motivation | Listening | Problem Solving | Communication | Understanding Needs | Selling | Self-Assessment |
|---|---|---|---|---|---|---|---|---|---|---|
| 31. Win–Win Solutions | * | | | * | * | | * | | * | * |
| 32. Build on the Customer's Proposal | * | | | | | | * | * | | * |
| 33. Being Creative | * | | * | * | | | | | * | * |
| 34. Tactfully Redirect | * | * | | | | * | * | | * | * |
| 35. How Not to Give Away the Shop | * | * | * | * | * | * | * | * | * | * |
| 36. Check Understanding | * | * | * | | * | * | * | * | * | * |
| 37. Standard Operating Procedure | | * | | | | * | | | | * |
| 38. Manage Expectations | * | | | | | * | * | | | * |
| 39. Helping Customers Be Profitable | * | | | | | | | * | * | * |
| 40. Putting Yourself into It | * | * | * | * | | | | | | * |
| 41. Take Action | * | | * | | | | * | | * | * |
| 42. Behavior Is What Customers Remember | | * | * | | | * | | | * | * |
| 43. When the Company Is Used as an Excuse for Bad Action | * | | | | * | | | | * | * |
| 44. Build on Satisfaction | * | | * | * | | * | * | | | * |
| 45. Who Benefits? | * | | | | | * | * | * | | * |
| 46. Be Helpful | * | * | * | | | | * | * | | * |
| 47. On the Front Line | * | * | | | * | * | * | * | | * |
| 48. Promises, Promises | * | * | | | * | | | | | * |
| 49. How to Handle an Unhappy Customer | | | * | | * | * | * | * | * | * |
| 50. How to Defuse Unhappy Customers | | | * | | * | * | * | * | * | * |
| 51. Venting | | | * | | * | * | * | * | * | * |
| 52. Ways to Overcome Barriers | | | | | * | * | * | * | | * |
| 53. The Irate Customer | | * | * | | * | * | * | | * | * |
| 54. Selling Skills | | * | * | | * | * | * | * | * | * |
| 55. Energy for Selling | | | * | | * | | * | | * | * |
| 56. The Telephone | | | * | | * | | * | * | * | * |
| 57. How to Transfer a Call | | | * | | * | * | * | | | * |
| 58. How to Take an Accurate Message | | | | | * | | * | * | | * |
| 59. Using the Phone with a Computer | | | * | | | | * | * | | * |
| 60. How to Avoid Stress and Burnout | | * | | | | * | * | | | * |

# The Customer
# Service
# Training
# Tool Kit

## Activity 1

# Why Should I Give Super Service?

What are the benefits of delivering Super Service from a customer service provider's point of view?

## Background and Purpose

Every organization knows the benefits of delivering Super Service. Too often, however, the people on the front line don't recognize these benefits because they don't seem to have anything to do with them specifically. This activity will help front line customer service providers understand the benefits of delivering Super Service from their own perspective. By working in teams, the participants will come up with many more benefits than they would individually.

## Objectives

By the end of this activity, participants will:

■ Understand the benefits of delivering Super Service from their own points of view.

■ Uncover other benefits they had not considered.

■ Look at their jobs from a different perspective.

■ Understand how these benefits apply to their personal lives.

## Time

Approximately 45 minutes

## Materials Required

1. Twelve 3×5-inch cards per participant

2. Exercise 1.1

## Mini Lecture

From a customer's point of view, delivering Super Service makes perfect sense. The customers get great service *even when they don't deserve it!* The benefits from the customer service provider's point of view are not always obvious. However, they are keys to making your life easier, more fun, and more meaningful.

## Steps to Follow

1. Hand out 3×5-inch cards so participants can write down the benefits.

2. Have each team brainstorm the benefits of delivering Super Service from their own point of view.

3. Ask teams to write down their top six benefits.

4. Invite each team to discuss its benefits with the entire group.

5. Distribute Exercise 1.1 and ask participants to complete it individually.

6. Provide a brief summary and answer any questions before wrapping up.

## Benefits to Look For

I experience being at my best when I deliver Super Service, because the person who receives the most service is me.

I am not at the mercy of my customers. It doesn't matter whether my customers deserve Super Service or not; by choosing to give it to them anyway, I remain in control of how I feel.

My life becomes easier, more fun, and more meaningful. When I feed the positive energy within me, it grows in all other aspects of my life, and positive energy attracts positive energy.

People notice that I do a great job and I become an asset. When I am tired of work I feel stuck in mental fatigue. If I change my attitude, my whole world is filled with new opportunities.

## Discussion Points

1. How did team members feel as the ideas were bounced around?

2. What benefits were most important?

3. How do these benefits affect (fit in with) the rest of their lives?

# EXERCISE 1.1: SUPER SERVICE ACTION PLAN

The actions I will take as a result of this activity are:

1. _____
   _____
   _____
   _____

2. _____
   _____
   _____
   _____

3. _____
   _____
   _____
   _____

4. _____
   _____
   _____
   _____

5. _____
   _____
   _____
   _____

6. _____
   _____
   _____

I will review this action plan on: _____    _____
                                      (date)                                    (signed)

## Background and Purpose

Super Service often occurs at the interface between company and customer. Too often, this interface creates problems and issues that are most strongly felt by the customer. Lack of proper procedures, unhelpful authority levels, and a discouraging management style only serve to make the interface more problematic.

The purpose of this activity is to help strengthen the interface between company and customer.

## Objectives

By the end of this activity, participants will be able to:

1. Understand the Moments of Truth in their jobs.

2. Determine how these moments are currently handled and how to move forward.

3. Turn every customer interaction into a positive event.

4. Set up a network of responsibility to deliver Super Service.

5. Develop an action plan to recommend to management.

## Time

Approximately 3 hours

## Materials Required

1. Flip chart and marking pens

2. Overhead projector and screen

3. Overheads 2.1, 2.2, and 2.3

4. Case Study 2.4

5. Exercises 2.5, 2.6, and 2.7

## Activity 2
# Moments of Truth

Connecting with a customer's heart and soul means appreciating your customers as fully rounded human beings with all the joy, family issues, money scares, and work problems that every one of us experiences from time to time.

# Mini Lecture

Your job is critically important to customer satisfaction. When you do a poor job, it has a domino effect until finally the customer suffers. The way to ensure Super Service is through a network of responsibility: Everyone knows that his or her job has a direct impact on somebody else's. Whether your job is to serve internal or external customers, you have the opportunity to interact with colleagues in a helpful manner.

Here's an example of how this works in an airline company:

*(If you have your own example, please use that.)*

- Managers serve the front-line service providers so that they in turn serve the passengers.

- Catering staff keep planes well stocked so the flight attendants can assist passengers.

- Maintenance workers make it possible for flights to take off on time.

Suppliers and customers "connect" at moments in time. These moments are called, Moments of Truth. Unfortunately, the last "connect" is often the only one customers remember! Even if the 99 previous "connects" were great, if the last one was a disaster, the disaster is the one people will remember!

# Steps to Follow

1. Show Overhead 2.1. Explain that even when you are not serving customers directly, you are always serving them indirectly.

2. Show Overhead 2.2. Explain the three characteristics: Empathy means showing customers that you care about their problems. Procedure means knowing the procedure and following it, while at the same time having some discretion built in to make decisions. Resolution means taking responsibility; "I will call you back with that answer."

3. Show Overhead 2.3. Explain the four keys for handling Moments of Truth: Know what your customers expect and supply it. Be willing to find a solution and ensure that the customer is satisfied. Follow set crisis management procedures, and help customers to meet their deadlines.

4. Divide participants into groups of four or six.

   a. Ask them to discuss times when they were suddenly let down by a supplier and to list characteristics that were present.

   b. Ask them to discuss times when a supplier resolved their problems and to list characteristics that were present.

   c. How did they feel about the suppliers in the different situations?

5. Distribute Case Study 2.4. Allow 10 minutes to review the case study.

6. Distribute Exercise 2.5. Allow 20 to 30 minutes to complete it. Use Facilitator Notes: Case Study to respond to questions and answers.

7. Distribute Exercise 2.6. Allow 20 to 30 minutes to complete it. Use the Discussion Points to elicit feedback.

8. Distribute Exercise 2.7. Ask participants to complete it individually.

9. Provide a summary and answer any questions before wrapping up.

## Discussion Points

1. Discuss participants' "moments of truth" (how or when their jobs impact the customer, either directly or through someone else).

2. Discuss the group's conclusions and record their answers on the flip chart.

3. How easy will it be to incorporate these ideas into everyday behavior?

4. Discuss with the group ways to improve each Moment of Truth.

5. Ask them to support each other via phone or E-mail, to remind them of learning points throughout the rest of the day, week, or month.

6. Restate the importance of interacting with colleagues and customers in a helpful manner.

# If you are not serving

# the customer,

# your job is to be serving

# someone who is.

# Three ways of handling Moments of Truth are:

■ **Empathy**

Show customers that you care about their problems.

■ **Procedure**

Follow procedure and have some discretion built in to make decisions.

■ **Resolution**

Take responsibility to resolve problems quickly and efficiently.

# Four keys to
# handling Moments of Truth are:

1. Meet the customers' performance standards. Know what your customers expect and supply it.

2. Own the problem. Be willing to find a solution and ensure that the customer is satisfied.

3. Understand and follow set crisis management procedures for handling problems. Follow the instructions that your company has provided.

4. Handle problems immediately. Help your customers meet their deadlines.

The following case study shows what happened to Cathy Pearl when she made a claim to her insurance company following an accident. At the end of the case study, you will be asked to identify the Moments of Truth and analyze how they were handled.

Cathy Pearl was driving to work in her Cadillac. It had been her father's car and was the only thing she had after he passed away. It was a fine, clear day and the visibility was excellent. She came to a complete halt at a Stop sign and was suddenly thrown forward in her seat as the car behind crashed into her.

Cathy was okay, apart from being badly shaken and having a sore neck. The other driver apologized and admitted he was at fault. Police verified this later. Unfortunately, the Cadillac was not driveable and was towed away.

Later that day, Cathy searched her policy for a claim form. There was none, and she could not understand the legalese in the policy. She contacted the insurance company. After many rings, the switchboard operator answered and asked Cathy to explain her problem. After explaining (including that the car was all she had after her father's death), she was put through to a claims clerk and she was asked for her policy number, address, and so on. She was transferred to a different claims clerk and asked for the same information again. She was told to submit a claim form. Cathy explained she did not have one. She was transferred to a third claims clerk for a forms request. Cathy told the clerk that she needed a car for work. The clerk said she must complete the claim form before anything could happen.

Five days later a claim form arrived. Cathy completed it and sent it back. She telephoned the company the next day. After twenty-two rings and giving an explanation to both the switchboard operator and claims clerk, Cathy reemphasized her need for a car to get to work. Cathy was told her car was a write-off.

The next day, an insurance agent called to tell Cathy she had one hour to clean her personal belongings out of the vehicle. The garage the Cadillac had been towed to was an hour from Cathy's office and she did not have a car. The agent told her it was not his problem—if the car was not cleaned out, she would lose everything in it!

Cathy borrowed a car from a friend and drove to where her Cadillac was. The same friend later told Cathy to ask for a replacement car. After calling the insurance agent twice, she was given a replacement car.

Three days later, Cathy called the insurance office again and after nineteen rings and twice being put on hold, the insurance agent told Cathy the car was worth $2,300. Cathy told the agent that she could never purchase the same car for that amount of money. She said she would not accept it. The agent said she had no alternative and that once she had the appraisal amount, the replacement car must be returned.

Cathy called an outside certified appraiser who valued the Cadillac at $3,750. Cathy said that she would have her lawyer speak to the insurance company. The battle is still going on.

During the middle of this crisis, Cathy received unsolicited mail from her insurance company, addressed to "Dear Motorist." It read in part: "You are our best customer…take out an insurance policy with us and you will always be number one!"

## EXERCISE 2.5

1. In the following columns, identify the main Moments of Truth from the case study. State how they were handled and what should have happened if the insurance company intended to fulfill its advertising promise.

| Moments of Truth | Interface: Good or Bad | How to Improve It |
|---|---|---|
|  |  |  |

2. How would Cathy have felt (circle one of the numbers below) about the insurance company after her...

|  | Dissatisfied | | Neutral | | Satisfied |
|---|---|---|---|---|---|
| • contact with the switchboard operator | 1 | 2 | 3 | 4 | 5 |
| • contact with claims people | 1 | 2 | 3 | 4 | 5 |
| • contact with insurance agent | 1 | 2 | 3 | 4 | 5 |

Why is that?

3. How would you rate the insurance company as a whole concerning the following three areas?

|  | Not Good | | Neutral | | Very Good |
|---|---|---|---|---|---|
| • empathy | 1 | 2 | 3 | 4 | 5 |
| • procedure | 1 | 2 | 3 | 4 | 5 |
| • resolution | 1 | 2 | 3 | 4 | 5 |

# FACILITATOR NOTES: CASE STUDY

Participants were asked to identify the main Moments of Truth from the case study and to state how they were handled and what should have happened if the insurance company intended to fulfill its advertising promise.

| Moments of Truth | Interface: Good or Bad | How to Improve It |
|---|---|---|
| No claim form | Bad | Include claim form in package |
| Policy presentation | Bad–Legalese, unclear | A short summary of main points |
| Contact with switchboard | Bad–Too many rings | Answer pleasantly after 3 rings |
| Contact with three different claims people | Bad–Too many times having to explain everything | Connect to appropriate clerk and explain the situation |
| Claim form late | Bad–Inefficient | Use express delivery |
| Contact switchboard and claims clerk | Bad–22 rings. No empathy re: her father's car being a write-off. | Use empathy and help provide replacement car for work |
| Contact insurance agent | Bad–No time, no understanding | Use empathy and allow time to clean out the car |
| Contact insurance agent | Bad–Not following policy rules | Provide replacement car |
| Contact insurance agent | Bad–17 rings and put on hold twice | Answer after 3 rings |
| Contact insurance agent | Bad–Car undervalued | Provide reasonable value |
| Mailer | Addressed to "Dear Motorist" | Do not send mailers to existing customers |

**EXERCISE 2.6**

1. List below some Moments of Truth in your company. How good or bad is the interface? What can be done to improve it? (Be prepared to discuss your answers with the group.)

| Moments of Truth | Interface: Good or Bad | How to Improve It |
|---|---|---|
|  |  |  |

If your company has many functions, concentrate on the functions that impact your job.

2. On a scale of 1 to 5, how do you think customers rate your company?

|  | Not Good |  | Neutral |  | Very Good |
|---|---|---|---|---|---|
| • empathy | 1 | 2 | 3 | 4 | 5 |
| • procedure | 1 | 2 | 3 | 4 | 5 |
| • resolution | 1 | 2 | 3 | 4 | 5 |

3. If your company scored 4 or 5 for any of the three items in question 2, give two recent examples.

4. If your company scored 1 or 2 for any of the three items in question 2, give two recent examples.

5. How could management help facilitate a better interface in Moments of Truth?

6.  What suggestions would you make to improve the network of responsibility to service?

7.  What actions will you take personally to improve your handling of Moments of Truth?

8.  What actions can you recommend to management so that Moments of Truth are handled better?

# EXERCISE 2.7: SUPER SERVICE ACTION PLAN

The actions I will take as a result of this activity are:

1. _____

_____

_____

_____

2. _____

_____

_____

_____

3. _____

_____

_____

4. _____

_____

_____

5. _____

_____

_____

6. _____

_____

_____

I will review this action plan on: _____    _____
(date)                              (signed)

## Activity 3
# How to Revitalize My Energy

## Background and Purpose

An important part of delivering Super Service is having the energy to communicate in a positive way with customers. Since our energy typically fluctuates throughout the day due to a variety of circumstances, the key is knowing how to revitalize energy at any part of the day. This activity gives practical examples on how to revitalize energy.

## Objectives

By the end of this activity, participants will be able to:

1. Understand a variety of ways to revitalize energy.

2. Choose the easiest and most enjoyable method for their specific situation.

3. Build on their strengths.

## Time

Approximately 20 minutes

## Materials Required

1. Flip chart and marking pens

2. Overhead projector and screen

3. Overhead 3.1

4. Exercise 3.2

## Mini Lecture

Delivering Super Service is more about you than about the actual service you provide. It doesn't matter how much the company puts into the product or service. When it comes to customer service, the one thing that makes a difference is you! When you are delivering service all day long, it is easy to become tired and feel a lack of energy, so it is important that you know how to revitalize your energy. Just as a car needs refueling to get anywhere, you need to know how to replenish your energy.

## Steps to Follow

1. Show Overhead 3.1. Explain that everyone responds differently to stimuli. This list is just a guideline for ways to revitalize energy. Ask them to choose one of the guidelines. Ask if they chose passive activities (like taking a deep breath) or action-oriented activities (like taking a walk).

2. Ask everyone to pair up and make a list of ten more ways they can revitalize their energy.

3. Have everyone share their ideas. Record each new idea on the flip chart. Ask each person to choose two main ideas to use for the rest of the day.

4. Distribute Exercise 3.2 and ask participants to complete it individually.

5. Provide a brief summary and answer any questions before wrapping up.

## Discussion Points

1. Does anyone use any of these methods now?

2. How easy will it be to incorporate these ideas into your day?

3. Restate the importance of revitalizing your energy.

# 10 Ways to Revitalize Your Energy

1. Take a short walk outside.

2. Leave yourself a great message on your answering machine.

3. Stretch your neck slowly from side to side.

4. Start a journal and write a page a day.

5. Write a letter to an old friend.

6. Tidy your desk or drawers.

7. Complete the sentence, "What I need to do to be happy is...."

8. Add a plant or a new photograph to your space.

9. Read a newspaper or an uplifting book.

10. Take a deep breath, hold it, and then breathe out, releasing all the tension.

# EXERCISE 3.2: SUPER SERVICE ACTION PLAN

The actions I will take as a result of this activity are:

1. _____
   _____
   _____
   _____

2. _____
   _____
   _____
   _____

3. _____
   _____
   _____

4. _____
   _____
   _____

5. _____
   _____
   _____

6. _____
   _____
   _____

I will review this action plan on: _____     _____
                                        (date)                    (signed)

## Background and Purpose

Every organization knows the benefits of delivering Super Service. Too often, however, the ones delivering the service do not enjoy the same benefits. Sometimes, they do not even perceive that there is a benefit for them.

The purpose of this activity is to help individuals see the benefit for them in delivering Super Service.

## Objectives

By the end of this activity, participants will be able to:

1. Understand where they are in the spectrum of Super Service.

2. Understand how Super Service is of benefit to them.

## Time

Approximately 45 minutes

## Materials Required

1. Flip chart and marking pens

2. Overheads 4.1 and 4.2

3. Exercise 4.3

## Mini Lecture

The first step toward any kind of change is awareness. We have to be aware of what needs to change before we can begin to change it. Think about yourself as a customer. Are you a great customer? Do you tell people exactly what it is you want or need? If you need help from a colleague, do you give clear instructions, expectations, and deadlines? If you want to be successful in your life, you must take care of yourself and your customers.

## Activity 4
# Super Service Self-Assessment

## Closed-Eye Process Instructions

Note to the facilitator: Speak in a soft, calming voice. Take your time and read the following instructions out loud to the participants.

Sit comfortably in your chair with your back straight, both feet on the floor, and your hands loosely in your lap. Close your eyes for a moment. Think about your customers (they can be internal or external customers). Pick one customer in particular. See yourself interacting with this customer. How do you look? Do you look peaceful or worried? How do you feel when you are with this customer? Do you feel calm or anxious? How do you feel about other customers that you interact with? Rub the side of your chair and open your eyes.

## Steps to Follow

1. Show Overhead 4.1: Self-Assessment Tool. Ask each participant to write down the five words that most clearly express how they feel about their customers.

2. Show Overhead 4.2: Self-Assessment Results. Ask participants to score themselves based on the Self-Assessment Results.

3. Group participants into teams of four. Explain that they will have 10 minutes to brainstorm ideas that will help them become more interested, empathetic, informed, and pleasant with their customers. *Tell the teams they will be asked to share their ideas.*

4. Ask teams to present their ideas, using the flip chart to write down key concepts. Use the discussion points below to elicit feedback.

5. Distribute Exercise 4.3 and ask participants to complete it as individuals.

6. Provide a brief summary and answer any questions before wrapping up.

## Discussion Points

1. Which key ideas will you use?

2. How can you support each other in implementing these ideas?

3. Restate the idea that if you want to be successful in your life, you must take care of your customers. Pay attention to small details; they cost less and they mean a lot.

## Self-Assessment Tool

Write down the five words that most clearly express how you feel about your customers:

| | | | |
|---|---|---|---|
| a. | Interested | Empathetic | Informed |
| b. | Problems | Issues | Jargon |
| c. | Thanks | Clarity | Acknowledgment |
| d. | Ignored | Disinterested | Unclear |
| e. | Green | Pleasant | Content |
| f. | Disturbed | Red | Unpleasant |

## Self-Assessment Results

1.  Each line has a letter beside it. Write down the letter next to each line that has a word circled.

2.  If three or more words appear on lines a, c, or e, *you enjoy interacting with your customers.*

3.  If three or more words appear on lines b, d, or f, *you do not enjoy interacting with your customers.*

# EXERCISE 4.3: SUPER SERVICE ACTION PLAN

The actions I will take as a result of this activity are:

1. _____

   _____

   _____

   _____

2. _____

   _____

   _____

   _____

3. _____

   _____

   _____

   _____

4. _____

   _____

   _____

   _____

5. _____

   _____

   _____

   _____

6. _____

   _____

   _____

   _____

I will review this action plan on: _____     _____
                                        (date)                              (signed)

## Activity 5

# How Do I Feel About My Customers?

Seeing the good in yourself and your circumstances is an important step in developing a positive attitude.

## Background and Purpose

This activity puts the roles of customer and service provider into perspective. We are all customers and all service providers at one time or another. When we think about how we like to be treated as customers, we become better service providers. The purpose of this activity, therefore, is to help service providers view their customers differently, to motivate and inspire customer service providers to feel great about their customers, and change from a self-focused attitude to a customer-focused attitude.

## Objectives

By the end of this activity, participants will be able to:

1. Understand their roles as service providers.

2. Gauge their attitude toward customers.

3. Learn techniques for developing a customer-oriented attitude.

## Time

Approximately 20 minutes

## Materials Required

1. Handouts 5.1 and 5.2

2. Exercise 5.3

## Mini Lecture

How you feel about your customers depends entirely on you. Your customers are people with the same concerns that you have: family issues, financial problems, work tensions, and so on. Every morning when you look at yourself in the mirror, you are seeing a customer. What kind of customer are you? How would you feel about serving someone like you?

Often, the way we interact with our customers is the same way we interact with everyone in our lives. Let's take a look at how you feel about your customers by doing a short exercise.

## Steps to Follow

1. Distribute Handout 5.1. Ask participants to complete the checklist.

2. Distribute Handout 5.2: Answers. (Notice that the answer to question 5 is missing.)

3. Reread question 5 out loud. Ask the participants to close their eyes. Give them 2 minutes with their eyes closed. Now ask them how it felt to be "on hold" for 2 minutes!

4. Ask participants to complete Exercise 5.3.

5. Provide a summary and answer any questions before wrapping up.

## Discussion Points

1. How did it feel to perceive the answers from a customer's perspective?

2. How often do you put yourself in the customers' shoes?

3. Brainstorm some ideas to help us remember that we are a reflection of our customers.

**HANDOUT 5.1**

## How You Feel about Your Customers

Read this checklist and circle your answers:

T = True or F = False.

1. T F   Customers want too much service.

2. T F   Customers need to understand my side of the story.

3. T F   Customers should not expect a fast response.

4. T F   Customers complain about insignificant problems.

5. T F   Placing a customer on hold for 2 minutes is
         acceptable.

6. T F   Telling the customer I handle lots of issues is okay.

7. T F   I need some appreciation from customers.

8. T F   Someone else should deal with irate customers.

## Answers—How You Feel about Your Customers

The answers are written as if you are the customer, so you will understand the point of view from a customer's perspective.

1. FALSE    Customers want too much service.

   *As a customer yourself, you want and expect good service.*

2. FALSE    Customers need to understand my side of the story.

   *As a customer, you are concerned with your own problems, especially if the service provider is responsible for them. You are not interested in the other side of the story.*

3. FALSE    Customers shouldn't expect a fast response.

   *As a customer, you may have tried to solve the problem yourself. By the time you've called the service provider, you've already spent too much time on it and you expect a fast response from the experts.*

4. FALSE    Customers complain about insignificant problems.

   *As a customer, no problem is too small, especially if it's creating frustration in your life. If someone says your problem is small and insignificant—how does that make you feel?*

5. TRUE    Placing a customer on hold for 2 minutes is acceptable.

   *The group will discuss the answer to this question.*

6. FALSE    Telling the customer I handle lots of issues is okay.

   *As a customer, I interpret this to mean that the product or service is prone to lots of problems—not good for long-term business.*

7. FALSE    I need some appreciation from customers.

   *What goes around does come around, and we all like appreciation. Often that appreciation comes from a different source. Customers are not always appreciative, even of good service; they expect it!*

8. FALSE    Someone else should deal with irate customers.

   *Have you ever been an irate customer? If so, you probably know that you are usually annoyed at the product or the company, not the person serving you. But if that person starts to take it personally, you feel the tension build. So, from either point of view, it doesn't work to take things personally.*

# EXERCISE 5.3: SUPER SERVICE ACTION PLAN

The actions I will take as a result of this activity are:

1. _____

_____

_____

_____

2. _____

_____

_____

_____

3. _____

_____

_____

4. _____

_____

_____

5. _____

_____

_____

6. _____

_____

_____

I will review this action plan on: _____     _____
                                       (date)                                         (signed)

## Background and Purpose

Most often, people think customers are outside the company. However, the customer is also the person who seeks help, information, or support from within the company. In other words, the customer can be the person in the next office.

## Objectives

By the end of this activity, participants will be able to:

1. Identify internal customers.

2. Understand how their job affects other people's jobs.

## Time

Approximately 45 minutes

## Materials Required

1. Flip chart and markers

2. Overhead 6.1

3. Handouts 6.2 and 6.3

4. Exercise 6.4

## Activity 6
# Identifying External and Internal Customers

## Mini Lecture

You know who your external customers are, but do you know your internal customers and how your job affects theirs? Internal customers include your boss, colleagues, peers, assistants, and different departments or locations. First, we are going to look at some affirmations. Affirmations help to provide you with a positive mental attitude.

## Steps to Follow

1. Show Overhead 6.1. These affirmations will help you with both external and internal customers. Notice the first one: *"My customer is anyone who isn't me."* Sometimes we don't know exactly who our customers

When you explain to customers *how* their service needs will be met by your organization, they feel in control.

are. If you have the attitude that everyone is a potential customer, you are putting yourself in a good frame of mind to be of service. Ask each participant to silently choose one of the affirmations. Explain that they can use this every day to remind them of what they most need to learn. The following is a list of key points that can be made about the affirmations:

a. Taking full responsibility means not saying you can do something that is impossible to do.

b. Keeping promises means being organized and having a system to remember what you said you would do.

c. Establishing good rapport does not take long. It can be done simply by asking, "How is it going for you?" and listening to the answer before moving on.

d. Listening often means paying attention to what's *not* being said.

e. Showing a desire to serve is a key to Super Service.

f. Posture transmits over telephone wires.

g. When you lower the prices of your products and services, customers expect you to do it every time.

h. Making eye contact does not mean staring people down; it means looking at someone with a steady gaze.

i. Having a positive attitude helps you and your customers.

j. Understand the customer's priorities and address those first.

k. Taking responsibility means saying, "I will do it."

2. Distribute Handout 6.2 and ask the participants to complete it. Explain that this is a checklist to see how they are doing with their Super Service attitude.

Debrief the exercise by stating the following key points:

a. If you have five or more "yes's," you are doing really well. If you have fewer than five, you may want to review some of your Super Service people skills.

b. Learning how to get along with others is a key to Super Service. Being open and willing helps people feel comfortable.

c. Being a considerate customer will help you understand the other side of the equation. When you are in a customer situation, look at how you behave and how other people provide you with Super Service.

d. Would you enjoy being served by someone like yourself? If not, what do you need to change?

3. Distribute Handout 6.3 and ask the participants to fill in the blanks. Key questions to ask are:

a. How many internal customers do you have? More or fewer than you thought?

b. How does your job affect theirs?

    c.   Have you ever asked them if there is anything you can do to make their jobs easier?

    d.   Do you know their priorities?

4.  Ask participants to complete Exercise 6.4. If you have time, use the discussion points below.

5.  Provide a summary and answer any questions before wrapping up.

## Discussion Points

1.  How do you feel about this exercise?

2.  What will you do differently?

3.  How can you change things on an ongoing basis?

# Super Service Affirmations

1. My customer is anyone who isn't me.
2. My customers are people first.
3. I am a great customer.
4. I take full responsibility to solve customer problems.
5. I keep all the promises I make to my customers.
6. I establish and maintain good rapport with customers.
7. I respect my customer's point of view.
8. I listen to understand how my customer feels.
9. I look beyond people's words to understand their feelings.
10. I always acknowledge what my customer is feeling.
11. I show a desire to serve.
12. I smile and maintain eye contact.
13. I sit straight and I stand straight.
14. I will not "give away the shop" to bribe my customer.
15. Every interaction is a positive attitude opportunity.
16. I control my biases and my judgments.
17. I show my customers that I care and am on their side.
18. I acknowledge my customers' priorities.
19. I take responsibility and use "I" instead of "we."
20. I connect with my customer's heart and soul.

# Action—How Am I Doing?

Read the following statements and circle "Yes" or "No."

| | | |
|---|---|---|
| Yes | No | I show a desire to serve. |
| Yes | No | I am a problem solver. |
| Yes | No | I recently helped solve a difficult problem. |
| Yes | No | I gather information well. |
| Yes | No | People understand the information I give. |
| Yes | No | I check for understanding. |
| Yes | No | People feel comfortable asking me for help. |
| Yes | No | I am a considerate customer. |
| Yes | No | I give more than I take. |
| Yes | No | I would enjoy being served by someone like me. |

**HANDOUT 6.3**

# Internal Customers

# How My Job Affects Theirs

_____

_____

_____

_____

_____

_____

_____

_____

# EXERCISE 6.4: SUPER SERVICE ACTION PLAN

The actions I will take as a result of this activity are:

1. _____
   _____
   _____
   _____

2. _____
   _____
   _____
   _____

3. _____
   _____
   _____
   _____

4. _____
   _____
   _____

5. _____
   _____
   _____

6. _____
   _____
   _____

I will review this action plan on: _____    _____
                                        (date)                          (signed)

## Background and Purpose

Every day we move between being served and providing service. The important part is how we do it. It is a choice. We decide what kind of script we write for ourselves: comedy, drama, tragedy, or romance. It doesn't matter which end of the service we are at; we still decide on the script.

It seems difficult to decide on a comic script when we feel depressed, but the key to this activity is understanding that it is still our choice. We are the directors; we choose how we want to play our parts.

## Objectives

By the end of this activity, participants will be able to:

1. Accept themselves as they are right now.

2. Do a great job even when they don't feel like it.

## Time

Approximately 20 minutes

## Materials Required

1. Flip chart and markers

2. Overhead 7.1

3. Handout 7.2

4. Exercise 7.3

## Mini Lecture

When we become conscious of other people, we can look for opportunities either to help or to hinder. When we turn toward helping others, it takes our focus away from our own problems and we begin to feel better about ourselves. This happens for a number of reasons, but the main ones are:

## Activity 7
# Serving Your Best When Feeling Your Worst

To serve others is ultimately to serve ourselves, because when we open our hearts, our spirit grows and becomes stronger.

a. By letting go of our problems, we show ourselves that we are in charge of our lives; this makes us feel empowered.

b. When we accept that we are the best we can be right now, we stop looking into the future for a better way of being and realize that we are the best right now!

Explain that when we take our minds into the past, we often feel guilty about what went wrong, what we did or did not do in a given situation. When we take our minds into the future, we worry about what will or will not happen. This is why it is so important to remain in the present.

Being present with the situation means letting go of the past and the future and being conscious of what is happening in the moment it is happening. When you can do this, you will find that the moment provides its own solutions.

## Steps to Follow

1. Show Overhead 7.1 and ask each participant to provide an idea of "Let go, let flow!" (Encourage ideas about letting go of problems, worries, and concerns. Guide the class toward remembering times when they felt everything was right in their lives, and how things seemed to work out easily.) Let go and let flow is about emptying the mind of all its clutter and being everything for the customer. It does not mean that we become like zombies; it means that we become present so that we can do the best job that is needed at the moment.

2. Provide the group with copies of Handout 7.2. Ask them to complete the evaluation.

3. Ask participants to complete Exercise 7.3.

4. Provide a summary and answer any questions before wrapping up.

## Discussion Points

1. What are some actions that will help you to think of other people and take your mind off your own problems?

   Examples: Send flowers, a card, or chocolates to a customer, coworker, or friend.

2. What are some actions that will allow you to feel better about yourself?

   Examples: Exercise, cook nourishing food.

3. What did you think of the handout? Have your answers made you feel any differently about how to Be Your Best, When Feeling Your Worst?

4. Suggest the following affirmation, to be repeated every day: "I am the best, and I'm getting better and better every day!"

# Let Go, Let Flow

**HANDOUT 7.2**

# Action—How Do I Let Go and Let Flow?

Answer each of the following questions in one sentence (ten words or less).

1. What is the main reason for me not to let go?

_____

_____

_____

2. What do I get to hold on to, by not letting go?

_____

_____

_____

3. How does not letting go keep me stuck?

_____

_____

_____

4. What have I let go of in the past?

_____

_____

_____

5. How do I feel when I let go?

_____

_____

_____

6. What will I let go of today?

_____

_____

_____

# EXERCISE 7.3: SUPER SERVICE ACTION PLAN

The actions I will take as a result of this activity are:

1. _____
_____
_____
_____

2. _____
_____
_____
_____

3. _____
_____
_____

4. _____
_____
_____

5. _____
_____
_____

6. _____
_____
_____

I will review this action plan on: _____    _____
                                         (date)                              (signed)

## Background and Purpose

Some people think that showing a desire to serve means being like a doormat, and let's face it, nobody wants to be a doormat. This activity provides people with a reason to serve. It shows that serving takes courage, power, leadership, and a strong spirit. It demonstrates that these skills can be learned and that they will enhance your personal life as well as your work life.

## Objectives

By the end of this activity, participants will be able to:

1. Understand that the benefit of serving others is ultimately to serve ourselves.

2. Understand the skills involved in providing Super Service.

## Time

Approximately 45 minutes

## Materials Required

1. Overhead 8.1

2. Handout 8.2

3. Exercise 8.3

## Mini Lecture

Showing a desire to serve requires developing a good attitude. When you feel great, it is easy; but when you feel depressed or are dealing with a problem, it seems difficult to have a great attitude. People in the public eye have to put smiles on their faces even when they are facing huge problems...and that takes power and leadership. The question is, do you want to be a leader of your own life?

This is where power comes in. Many people think that the only power we have is over other people; but real

# Activity 8

# How to Show a Desire to Serve

What are the benefits of delivering Super Service from a customer service provider's point of view?

power is the power we have over ourselves. Imagine the power you would have if you could change a bad day into a good day, if you could think, "This problem can wait; right now I will serve my customer and do a great job." When you can do that, everything changes...even your problem.

Leaders decide that they have the strength to serve, and so can you. It's all in your attitude. You can have a great attitude and feel good about your life, or you can have a bad attitude and feel awful. It's a choice—your choice!

## Steps to Follow

1. Show Overhead 8.1.

    a. Control your attitude—become like an actor. Think of a person with a great attitude and pretend to be like that person.

    b. Let anger go. Anger is poisonous and feeds upon itself. Let the anger go for now; you can always revisit it later if you need to.

    c. Maintain a positive attitude—think good thoughts. Do the right things. Make the best choices.

    d. Affirm your day. Every morning, look into the mirror and say, "Today is going to be a great day. I am going to be the best for myself and for my customers!"

2. Breath Control Exercise: Ask participants to take a deep breath and to hold it for a count of three. **Slowly** let the breath go for a count of six. Repeat for a count of four holding and eight breathing out. Feel the tension release with the breath. Explain that they can do the same with anger: They can let go of anger with an exhalation of breath. *Stress that they should not do this in front of a customer!*

3. Distribute Handout 8.2 and, after participants have completed the exercise, ask for feedback.

4. Distribute Exercise 8.3 and ask participants to complete it individually.

5. Provide a summary and answer any questions before wrapping up.

## Discussion Points

1. How do you feel about saying an affirmation each morning? What would it be?

2. Have you used breath control before to help release tension or anger? How did it feel?

3. How do you feel about using a positive person in your life as an example?

## How to Show a Desire to Serve

- Be in Control of Your Attitude

- Let Your Anger Go

- Maintain a Positive Attitude

- Affirm Your Day

**HANDOUT 8.2**

## Action—How to Show a Desire to Serve

1. Think of one person with a positive attitude and write down his or her name.

_____

2. In ten words or fewer, describe what makes that person have a positive attitude.

_____

_____

_____

_____

_____

3. List the positive attributes of this person that you can use for yourself.

_____

_____

_____

_____

_____

# EXERCISE 8.3: SUPER SERVICE ACTION PLAN

The actions I will take as a result of this activity are:

1. _____
   _____
   _____
   _____

2. _____
   _____
   _____
   _____

3. _____
   _____
   _____

4. _____
   _____
   _____

5. _____
   _____
   _____

6. _____
   _____
   _____

I will review this action plan on: _____     _____
                                       (date)                                     (signed)

## Activity 9

# Who Teaches Me Super Service?

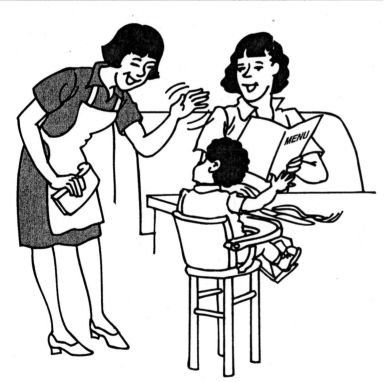

Connecting with a customer's heart and soul means appreciating your customers as fully rounded human beings with all the joy, family issues, money scares, and work problems that every one of us experiences from time to time.

## Background and Purpose

It can be difficult for an organization to see itself from the customers' perspective, and even more difficult for an individual to do it. If the company or individual does not acknowledge or distinguish between the things that work and the things that don't, the problems will continue.

The process has to start somewhere...and in this activity it begins with individuals seeing themselves more clearly and deciding what works and what does not work.

## Objectives

By the end of this activity, participants will be able to:

1. Identify the key steps in seeing ourselves clearly.

2. Acknowledge who they really are.

3. Identify their teachers.

4. Make an action plan to move forward.

## Time

Approximately 45 minutes

## Materials Required

1. Overhead 9.1

2. Handout 9.2

3. Exercise 9.3

## Mini Lecture

Super Service is not about changing who you are. It is about enhancing the parts of you that make your life work. One of the keys is to see yourself as others see you. The way to do this is to acknowledge everyone as your teacher, and turn every situation into a learning situation.

Most people are not alike. This is a good thing because if we were all the same, life would be very boring, and we would not last very long as a species. We need the variety: the thinkers, the doers, the inventors, the sports people, even the couch potatoes.

The way to step outside yourself is to see yourself in others and to see others in you. When you can accept that we are all human beings trying to get along as best we can, then you can truly be of service to others.

## Steps to Follow

1. Show Overhead 9.1. Explain that we are all teachers, and that every situation is a learning situation.

   Discuss the concept that, every time we dislike a certain type of person, we are really saying that we dislike a certain part of ourselves. Explain that if we get angry with someone, it is usually because we are angry at some part of ourselves or our lives that is not working. It is important when we are interacting with a customer to detach from our emotions and not to get angry.

2. Distribute Handout 9.2 and ask participants to complete it as individuals. Use the Discussion Points to generate group interaction.

3. Distribute Exercise 9.3 and ask participants to complete it.

4. Provide a summary and answer any questions before wrapping up.

## Discussion Points

1. Does everyone acknowledge teachers in our lives? Are there more than one?

2. Do we have to be in close personal contact with a person for that person to become one of our teachers? (No, we can even learn from teachers we may never get to see.)

- Everyone is my teacher.

- I learn from everyone around me.

- I am awake and help others to awaken.

- I am open to every different kind of person.

- I see the potential in everyone.

- I value serving others.

- I understand that what I do not like in others is usually what I do not like in myself.

**HANDOUT 9.2**

## Who Are My Teachers?

Take a few moments to fill in the blanks:

1. My main teacher is called _____

2. This person teaches me how to _____

3. My second teacher is called _____

4. This person reminds me to be more _____

5. My third teacher is called _____

6. I have noticed this person is very good at _____

7. I will use the information I have learned from my teachers to become more_____

_____

_____

_____

_____

# EXERCISE 9.3: SUPER SERVICE ACTION PLAN

The actions I will take as a result of this activity are:

1. _____

   _____

   _____

   _____

2. _____

   _____

   _____

   _____

3. _____

   _____

   _____

   _____

4. _____

   _____

   _____

   _____

5. _____

   _____

   _____

6. _____

   _____

   _____

I will review this action plan on: _____    _____
                                         (date)                          (signed)

## Background and Purpose

Every motivational speaker who believes in developing a positive mental attitude talks about the power of affirmations. This very quick game will help participants realize the importance of affirmations and choose one for themselves. It can relate to any part of their lives, whether personal or at work. The important thing is for them to develop the habit of using it every day.

## Objectives

By the end of this activity, participants will be able to:

1. Understand what affirmations are and the power of using them.

2. Choose a personal affirmation to use each day.

## Time

Approximately 20 minutes

## Materials Required

1. Overhead 10.1

2. Handout 10.2

3. Exercise 10.3

## Mini Lecture

Affirmations have been used since ancient times. They affirm the things we want to happen in our lives. They help us to distinguish the important things from the unimportant things. They help us to set goals.

If you speak the same affirmation every day for over three months, you will experience a change in your life. Affirmations work!

## Activity 10
# Affirmations

Incorporate the customer's ideas into your solution.

## Steps to Follow

1. Show Overhead 10.1. Ask participants if they have ever used affirmations before. Have they worked? How does it feel to have an affirmation? Is it something they will use now?

2. Distribute Handout 10.2. Ask for any participants to share their answers. Use the Discussion Points to help generate feedback and interactive discussion.

3. Distribute copies of Exercise 10.3. Ask participants to complete it and then ask for feedback.

4. Provide a summary and answer any questions before wrapping up.

## Discussion Points

1. Have you every used affirmations before?

2. What has worked or not worked?

3. Does this seem doable?

## Affirmation List

- I will be kind, loving, and generous.

- Today will be the best day of my life.

- Today I will make a positive difference.

- Today I will create my world the way I want it.

- Every day, I am getting better.

**HANDOUT 10.2**

## What Is My Affirmation?

Take a few moments to fill in the blanks:

My main goal in life is _____

_____

How I will accomplish this is to _____

_____

_____

Things I want to create in my life are _____

_____

_____

My affirmation is _____

_____

_____

## EXERCISE 10.3: SUPER SERVICE ACTION PLAN

The actions I will take as a result of this activity are:

1. _____

   _____

   _____

   _____

2. _____

   _____

   _____

   _____

3. _____

   _____

   _____

4. _____

   _____

   _____

5. _____

   _____

   _____

6. _____

   _____

   _____

I will review this action plan on: _____        _____
                                          (date)                              (signed)

# Activity 11
# How to Take Responsibility

## Background and Purpose

Most problems begin with people, and most problems end with people. If all people in an organization took responsibility for their actions, there would be far fewer problems. This activity creates an environment for looking at areas of responsibility.

Being responsible really means having the ability to respond to situations and people. What are you responsible for? What tools do you need to help you to be more responsible? How is responsibility affecting your work and life?

## Objectives

By the end of this activity, participants will be able to:

1. Understand the concept of responsibility.

2. Define the areas in their jobs that demand responsibility.

3. Learn basic ideas for accepting and working with responsibility.

## Time

Approximately 1 hour 20 minutes

## Materials Required

1. Overhead 11.1, 11.4, and 11.5.

2. Demonstration 11.2. (You must read the instructions before giving the demonstration.)

3. A flip chart marker or pen for Demonstration 11.2

4. Exercise 11.3.

5. Exercise 11.6.

## Mini Lecture

Taking responsibility at work begins by taking responsibility for yourself. It starts with small things: being on time, taking care of your appearance, keeping up your energy, getting along with other people, smiling, and maintaining eye contact. If you are doing these things now, then you are on the right track for being responsible.

The real test comes when you are called upon to give something extra, such as time, effort, or initiative. When a problem comes along, do you take ownership of it, or do you pass it along to someone else?

If you come from a positive point of view, you are more likely to be responsible for your own actions; if you come from a negative point of view, you are more likely to pass problems along for other people to solve. Do you view life as half full or half empty? If you understand that you are responsible for how you view the world, you will begin to see that being responsible puts you in the driver's seat; and if you're the driver, you can go wherever you want to go.

## Steps to Follow

1. Show Overhead 11.1. Explain that you can see life as either half full or half empty.

2. Ask for a volunteer to help you with Demonstration 11.2. Read the rules and perform the scenario. After you have finished, ask the participants to pair up and role play the three different attitudes: negative, positive, and neutral. When they have finished, ask them for feedback about what they learned. Ask them how they can relate this to their jobs.

3. Ask participants to complete Exercise 11.3. Emphasize that they should think of every aspect of their jobs over which they have responsibility.

4. Show Overheads 11.4 and 11.5. Explain that being responsible means taking right action in a timely manner. Emphasize the importance of following company instructions, and stress that sometimes there may be a need to improvise, so long as it is within the rules.

5. Group the participants into teams of 3 to 4. Then ask each person in turn to take 5 minutes to discuss a main responsibility with the group, in terms of what is working, what is not working, and what ideas the group has for making it work even better. Tell the groups that they should direct their solutions toward working smarter, not harder.

6. Debrief the exercise by asking: What did you learn? How do you feel about this exercise?

7. Ask participants to complete Exercise 11.6.

8. Provide a summary of the activity by reemphasizing the need to take responsibility for our work and ourselves. Ask if there are any questions.

# ATTITUDE

■ Do you view your life as half full or half empty?

■ If you are given a problem, do you look for a solution or feel overwhelmed?

■ Do you feel in control of your life, or feel that life is controlling you?

# DEMONSTRATION 11.2: WHO IS RESPONSIBLE FOR HOW YOU FEEL?

Have a volunteer help you with this demonstration.

1. You will need one flip chart marker (or pen) for this demonstration.

2. Ask the volunteer to hand you the flip chart marker.

3. Take the marker and demonstrate a negative response. For example: "Why did you give me this marker? It's not the right color! It smells strange! This marker is too big. It doesn't feel right and I think it will bleed through to the other pages. I hate this marker. I wish you hadn't given it to me!"

4. Hand the marker back to the volunteer and ask him or her to hand it to you once more. Emphasize to the participants that it is exactly the same marker.

5. Take the marker and demonstrate a positive response. For example: "This is a great marker. It's exactly the right color, and it even smells good! It's just the right size too. I think this marker is going to do a great job for me. I love this marker. Thank you for giving it to me!"

6. Now hand the marker back to the volunteer and ask him or her to hand it to you for a third time. Emphasize that it is exactly the same marker.

7. Take the marker and demonstrate a neutral response. For example: "A marker. Seems okay to me. Thank you."

8. Now ask the participants, what made the difference in each of these demonstrations?

9. Emphasize that the only difference was **attitude**! Same marker, different attitude. Explain that it was your choice to use a negative, positive, or neutral response.

10. Have participants pair up and repeat the exercise with each other, using anything they have—pen, pencil, pad of paper, or paper clip.

## EXERCISE 11.3: WHAT ARE YOU RESPONSIBLE FOR?

Take a moment to write down a list of all your responsibilities in the workplace:

- _____

- _____

- _____

- _____

- _____

- _____

- _____

- _____

- _____

- _____

- _____

- _____

- _____

- _____

Go back over your list and number your responsibilities in order of importance, number one being the most important.

## RESPONSIBILITY = RESPONSE

**Taking responsibility is all about your response to a situation. Here are some guidelines:**

- Be confident: "I can do this!"

- Sound responsive: "I will do this!"

- Show urgency: "I will take care of it right away!"

- Follow the company instructions: But be ready to improvise (within the rules) if necessary!

# HOW TO TAKE RESPONSIBILITY

1. Make "I" statements: "I will call the service department and get back to you by this afternoon."

2. Complete incompletes: Make a list of things you need to complete…then complete them.

3. Take notes: Write down what you intend to do and then do it.

4. Keep your word: Keep your word, and people will keep their word with you.

# EXERCISE 11.6: SUPER SERVICE ACTION PLAN

The actions I will take as a result of this activity are:

1. _____

_____

_____

_____

2. _____

_____

_____

_____

3. _____

_____

_____

4. _____

_____

_____

5. _____

_____

_____

6. _____

_____

_____

I will review this action plan on: _____      _____
                                          (date)                            (signed)

## Background and Purpose

The purpose of this activity is to clear a space for new things to happen. If a container is full, it cannot accept anything else. The same is true of you at work. If there is no space for you to maneuver, then everything will stay blocked. Clearing a space can help you feel cleaner, more refreshed, and more alive, ready to make a new start.

## Objectives

By the end of this activity, participants will be able to:

1. Clean up their workspace.

2. Understand what work is important and what is not.

3. Create a space for new habits to form.

## Time

Approximately 20 minutes

## Materials Required

1. Overhead 12.1

2. Exercises 12.2 and 12.3

## Mini Lecture

Shakespeare said that life is a stage and we are all players upon that stage. Imagine if our stage was so cluttered with props that we cannot move around. That's what we work with sometimes; desks that are so cluttered we cannot find anything on them, files on the floor, bookshelves overflowing with books we will never read.

In the Chinese art of placement, great care is taken to keeping your house or office tidy and in good working condition. The energy that circulates through your space affects how you feel. If you wake up in the morning and your bedroom is cluttered, or you

# Activity 12
# Clear a Space in My Life

have dusty piles of things under your bed, you are unconsciously bringing garbage into your life.

If you work on the telephone and talk to customers all day and your telephone is dirty, guess what is being transmitted along with your words? Today we will write down a list of things you don't need in your workspace.

## Steps to Follow

1. Show Overhead 12.1 and explain the concept of working and living in a clear space.

2. Ask participants to complete Exercise 12.2. Emphasize that they should use this exercise as a scheduling tool for clearing a space in their lives.

3. Debrief by asking "How do you feel? How long will it take to complete? What assistance do you need?"

4. Ask each person to find a partner. Tell the partners to exchange phone numbers and for the next four weeks (longer or shorter depending on the needs of the participants), they should support each other by finding out where they are in the project, how they are feeling, and what help (if any) they need.

5. Hand out Exercise 12.3 and ask participants to complete it.

6. Provide a summary and answer any questions before wrapping up.

# CLEAR A SPACE IN YOUR LIFE

1. Make your bed every day.

2. Clean a space a week (closet, kitchen, bathroom, etc.).

3. Give old things to the Salvation Army (or another good cause).

4. Throw broken things out.

5. Let go of old stuff that you no longer use.

# EXERCISE 12.2: CLEAR A SPACE FOR YOUR LIFE

In the space below, make a list of the top five areas in your life that need clearing out:

1._____

2._____

3._____

4._____

5._____

Starting with the most important area, make a list of all the things that are necessary, and all the things that you have not used for six months or more (and are unnecessary).

**Things that are necessary:**                           **Things that are unnecessary:**

_____                           _____

_____                           _____

_____                           _____

_____                           _____

_____                           _____

_____                           _____

_____                           _____

_____                           _____

# EXERCISE 12.3: SUPER SERVICE ACTION PLAN

The actions I will take as a result of this activity are:

1. _____
   _____
   _____
   _____

2. _____
   _____
   _____
   _____

3. _____
   _____
   _____
   _____

4. _____
   _____
   _____
   _____

5. _____
   _____
   _____
   _____

6. _____
   _____
   _____
   _____

I will review this action plan on: _____     _____
                                        (date)                          (signed)

## Background and Purpose

This activity is not only helpful at work; it also helps in your personal life. We often think we can get away with saying things so that we look good. The problem is that most of us recognize (if not immediately, then eventually) the people who do not walk their talk.

## Objectives

By the end of this activity, participants will be able to:

1. Understand the concept and importance of doing what they say they will do.

2. Learn, from examples, how a small interaction can make a big difference.

## Time

Approximately 2 hours

## Materials Required

1. Overhead 13.1

2. Exercise 13.2

3. Check-In Exercise 13.3

4. Exercise 13.4

## Mini Lecture

We used to think that we could dump toxic chemicals into the deepest part of the ocean and they would disappear for good. Now we know better; every action has a result. Everything we say creates an effect. When we say we will do something and we do not do it, somebody has to clean up the mess.

The difference between successful and unsuccessful companies is not so much in their products, systems, and facilities; it is in their people. It is the individual who makes the difference. If you want to work for a successful company

---

## Activity 13
# How to Walk My Talk

and be successful in your life, you have to commit yourself to providing the highest possible level of service in every aspect of your work. That begins with the understanding that *your word is law.*

## Steps to Follow

1. Show Overhead 13.1. Explain that if you say you will do something and then don't do it, your word is still law, and the law is that, "You do not keep your word." When you say, "I'll have this to you by Monday," does your mind already know that it's a toss of the coin whether it will be ready by Monday? Could it just as easily be Tuesday or Wednesday?

   Emphasize that walking your talk does not mean beating yourself up if you make a mistake. It means "upping" your game, being more aware of how your actions affect all those around you and, more importantly, yourself.

2. Group participants into twos, threes, or fours. Hand out copies of Exercise 13.2 and give each group 30 minutes to complete it.

3. Working through scenes 1 to 6, ask different groups to provide their answers. Discuss each of their answers with the rest of the participants.

4. Hand out Check-In Exercise 13.3 and ask each individual to complete it.

5. Hand out Exercise 13.4. Ask each individual to complete it.

6. Ask if there are any questions before providing a summary and wrapping-up.

Answers to look for in Exercise 13.2:

Scene 1.    In ending 1, the owner blames the seating problem on the other patrons. In ending 2, the party of five feel the owner has their interests at heart. He wants them to enjoy their evening and takes responsibility for seating them as quickly as possible. He also offers a complimentary drink so they are not left standing or having to pay for a drink at the bar to cover the restaurant's reservation error.

Scene 2.    In ending 1, the technician is unhelpful and makes the customer feel that he is too rushed to do a good job. In ending 2, the customer understands that the technician went the extra mile to do a good job. She will feel comfortable calling on the company again and buying more products from them.

Scene 3.    In ending 1, the salesperson doesn't care about the customer and just wants to make an easy sale. In ending 2, the salesperson asks questions to find out which is the best car for their needs.

Scene 4.    In ending 1, the bagger is just doing a job. In ending 2, the bagger explains why the two bags are necessary and how double bagging will help and protect the customer.

Scene 5.    In ending 1, the bank teller is saying the right things. In ending 2, the bank teller is actually looking out for the customer's interests.

Scene 6.    In ending 1, the mechanic is just doing his job. In ending 2, the mechanic has taken the time to change valves that could cause a problem. He lets the customer know that he has taken the time. This gives the customer reassurance that the mechanic has done and will do a thorough job.

## Discussion Points

1. Discuss the participants' answers in relation to costs and benefits to the company, the customers, and themselves.

2. Ask participants how they can use the information learned from this exercise to enhance their own job situations.

# WALK YOUR TALK

## Think before you agree to do something:
*"Can I **really** get this done?"*

## Do what you say you will do:
*"My word is law!"*

## Someone will have to clean it up:
*"If I don't do what I say, someone else
will have to do it for me!"*

# EXERCISE 13.2: WALKING THE TALK OF CUSTOMER SERVICE

Here are six scenes from a variety of customer situations. Each scene has two alternative endings. Compare the two and state which one would satisfy the customer more and why. Finally, identify what caused the two endings to be so different.

| Scene | Situation | Ending 1 | Ending 2 | Notes |
|-------|-----------|----------|----------|-------|
| 1. | A party of five has booked a table at an expensive restaurant. When they arrive, the owner apologizes and tells them it will be another 15 to 20 minutes. | The owner tells them that it was not the restaurant's fault; all the parties are taking their time this evening. Would they please wait at the bar?<br><br>They do not see the owner again. | The owner expresses concern for their evening plans. He tells them that he will personally overlook the tables and ensure they get seated as soon as possible. Meanwhile, would they care to enjoy a complimentary drink at the bar?<br><br>After 5 minutes, the owner checks on their comfort. Five minutes later he tells them they will be seated in 5 minutes. Five minutes later, he seats them. In front of the group, he tells the waiter to take good care of them. At the end of the evening, he checks to makes sure they enjoyed their meal. | |
| 2. | A technician finishes a service call on a washing machine for a busy mother of three small children. The technician says… | "If you sign here I'll be on my way. You should probably change the filter and get someone to tighten up the door. It's not a big deal, and I would do it myself, but it's not under warranty, plus I've got another ten customers to see this morning." | "I fixed the problem and the machine is working well now. I also changed the filter and tightened up the door so it doesn't squeak anymore. It only took a second. Here's my card; please call again if you have any problems. Your warranty is good for another year." | |

| Scene | Situation | Ending 1 | Ending 2 | Notes |
|---|---|---|---|---|
| 3. | A husband and wife are looking at a car with a salesperson. They are having a lot of difficulty deciding between a two-door and a four-door model. The salesperson says… | "This two-door model has a manufacturer's discount right now. It's a bargain. I'd go for this one!" | "Perhaps if you describe how you want to use the car, I might be able to make some suggestions. There are advantages and disadvantages to both types of vehicle, and my experience is that your needs determine your final choice." | |
| 4. | A woman in a supermarket buys a bottle of bleach and some groceries. The bagger says… | "Do you want paper or plastic?" He hands her two bags, one (double bagged) with the bleach in and one with the groceries. | "I'm going to double bag the bleach separately to keep it safe. We don't want it to break in the parking lot." | |
| 5. | A young man goes to the bank as he has been doing every month for two years, to cash his paycheck. He transfers 10 percent to a savings account. The bank teller says… | "Thank you. It's a lovely day today, isn't it. Here is your deposit slip. How do you want the cash? Have a nice day." | "Thank you. I notice that you are a regular saver with our bank. Have you seen our new account specially designed for regular savers? You can switch and earn a higher interest rate if you would like. Thank you, and how would you like the cash? Have a nice day." | |
| 6. | A motorcyclist is picking up his motorbike from routine servicing. The mechanic gives the motorbike to the customer and says… | "See you next season. Drive carefully." | "Everything looks fine. We checked the oil, the brakes, and the gears. We replaced a couple of valves that looked a bit worn. They might have lasted through the season, but we don't take any chances here. See you next season. Drive carefully." | |

## EXERCISE 13.3: CHECK-IN

Put this list near your desk and personalize it by adding your own:

1. I always think about what I am about to say before I say it.

2. Before I speak, I think, "Is it necessary; is it kind; is it wise?"

3. If I must talk about someone, I imagine the person is present.

4. People can count on me. I always do what I say I will do.

5. I complete all my tasks as quickly as possible.

6. I put my "busy" work aside to get on with the real job.

7. I arrive 10 minutes early to places so that I am on time.

8. I lighten myself up by consciously thinking about myself less.

9. I communicate clearly the purpose of my needs.

10. I make wise decisions and good choices.

11. _____

12. _____

13. _____

14. _____

15. _____

# EXERCISE 13.4: SUPER SERVICE ACTION PLAN

The actions I will take as a result of this activity are:

1. _____
   _____
   _____
   _____

2. _____
   _____
   _____
   _____

3. _____
   _____
   _____

4. _____
   _____
   _____

5. _____
   _____
   _____

6. _____
   _____
   _____

I will review this action plan on: _____    _____
                                              (date)                                      (signed)

# Activity 14
# The Right Attitude

Seeing the good in yourself and your circumstances is an important step in developing a positive attitude.

## Background and Purpose

Everything begins with attitude. If you are in "the flow," your job will run more smoothly and you will find it more enjoyable. Keeping this flow smooth and free flowing will help you and your customer by lessening the conflict and anxiety caused by a bad attitude.

This activity is designed to show the participants that the only difference between having a good attitude and a bad attitude is the choice we make. The other important thing about attitude is that it's infectious. If someone has a bad attitude in an office, it can actually have the effect of poisoning the entire office. On the other hand, if someone has a good attitude, it can lift everyone's spirits.

## Objectives

By the end of this activity, participants will be able to:

1. Understand the importance of having a good attitude.

2. Recognize how far-reaching the effects of a person's attitude can be.

3. Learn tools that will enhance our ability to make the "right attitude choice."

## Time

Approximately 1 hour

## Materials Required

1. Overheads 14.1, 14.3, and 14.5

2. Case Study 14.2

3. Exercise 14.4

4. Exercise 14.6

## Mini Lecture

You might think that having the right attitude means adding lots of things to our personality. However, having the right attitude means taking away, not adding to. It begins with emptying our minds so that we can be present with the customer. This does not mean that we become like zombies; it simply means we get rid of the clutter and the hustle and bustle that goes on in our heads, just for the moment that we are listening to our customer. Don't worry about your head being empty forever; it will fill up again very quickly with lists, projects, goals, forecasts, and so on.

## Steps to Follow

1. Show Overhead 14.1. Explain that we always make a difference. We need to be conscious of making the "right" difference.

2. Hand out Case Study 14.2. Ask each participant to read and respond to the questions. Ask for feedback from the participants and invite a general discussion. Ask if anyone had ever experienced anything like this.

3. Show Overhead 14.3. Explain that it is impossible to change other people. We want to believe we can…but we can't.

4. Ask participants to complete Exercise 14.4. This exercise is a way of monitoring the participants' attitudes and showing them where they can make improvements.

5. Show Overhead 14.5. Attitude is everything. The ways to improve your attitude all come from within you—it's a conscious choice.

6. Ask participants to complete Exercise 14.6.

7. Ask if anyone has final questions. Provide a final summary and wrap-up.

Answers to look for in Case Study 14.2.

1. What did the insurance agent, Bill Blunt, do wrong?

   - Bill does not answer the phone promptly and keeps Sandy waiting.

   - He then puts his hand over the receiver and continues his conversation.

   - He is showing Sandy that she is not important.

   - He did not take her policy number down when she first said it. If he had, he would have known her last name without asking her for it and asking for her to repeat the policy number.

   - He displayed the attitude that Sandy did not need to know the details.

2. What was the effect on Sandy, the customer?

   - Sandy felt unacknowledged as a customer.

   - Her needs were not met in any way.

3. Why did Bill Blunt behave that way?

- This is pure speculation, but one can only assume that Bill is overworked. He is disorganized and he doesn't have a good staff (they argue with him when he's on the phone).

4. What did Sandy want from the insurance agent?

   - Immediate attention, courtesy, and confidence in Bill as an insurance agent who has her best interests at heart.

5. What could Bill have done to satisfy Sandy's requirements?

   - Picked up the phone on the first couple of rings.

   - Looked up her name from the policy number and made her feel like an important customer (after all, she had been with him for over ten years!).

   - Listened to her needs and acknowledged her as a customer.

# IF WE THINK

# WE COULD HAVE MADE

# A DIFFERENCE,

# WE PROBABLY COULD HAVE!

# CASE STUDY 14.2: THE INSURANCE AGENT

Bill Blunt is a small insurance agent in a medium-sized town. Sandy calls on the phone. She has been Bill's customer for over ten years, although she never hears from him unless the rates change. Recently Bill sent her literature saying that the rates were going up and that she should buy a 20-year fixed-rate policy.

The phone rings about six times. Finally, someone picks it up and puts his or her hand over the receiver and continues speaking to someone else. After a couple of minutes, Sandy hears a voice say, "Bill Blunt!"

"Bill, this is Sandy. You seem very busy; do you have a minute?"

"Yes, just a minute, though."

"My policy number is 22045. I'm calling about the rate changes you sent me and to talk about the 20-year fixed-rate policy."

"Sandy who?"

"Sandy Harris."

"And your policy number is...?"

"22045."

"Ah, yes. You just need some blood work done to qualify. I talked with your husband last week. I'll set up a time for the nurse to come to your home and draw blood."

"Bill, I'm not ready to do that yet. I've noticed that we will be paying $500 more for the first year on this new policy. We might as well wait until our old policy expires."

"No, you don't want to do that. Now, when is a good time for the nurse to come?"

"Bill you're not listening to me. I need to know why it should be worth our while to pay $500 more for this policy."

"Sandy, I talked to your husband about this. I explained everything to him. He agrees, and all I need is a day and time that is convenient for the nurse to come. If you don't get the blood work done, you will miss the window of opportunity!"

"Then I guess we will just have to miss it then. Thanks, Bill. Goodbye!"

1. What did the insurance agent, Bill Blunt, do wrong?


2. What was the effect on Sandy, the customer?


3. Why did Bill Blunt behave that way?


4. What did Sandy want from the insurance agent?


5. What could Bill have done to satisfy Sandy's requirements?

# A BAD ATTITUDE

# IS EASY TO TURN AROUND IF

# YOU ARE THE ONE WITH IT...

# BUT IF YOU ARE ON THE

# RECEIVING END,

# IT IS VIRTUALLY IMPOSSIBLE

# TO TURN IT AROUND!

## EXERCISE 14.4: REVIEW

### Personal Improvement Plan

Put yourself in your customer's shoes. What kind of attitude do you normally display? In the space below, write a brief description of your attitude with customers (internal or external). How does your face look? How does your body language appear to others? Use some adjectives to describe your attitude, such as upbeat, cheerful, happy, sad, miserable, smiling, unhappy. Describe your body language in terms like slumped, upright, straight, tall, small, bent. Choose your own words:

My normal attitude is:_____

_____

_____

My usual body language that expresses my attitude is:_____

_____

_____

My tone of voice usually demonstrates that I am:_____

_____

_____

Now review the answers you gave above and ask yourself:

What are the positive ways that I can either improve my attitude or make my attitude even better?

_____

_____

_____

_____

## Ways to improve your attitude:

■ Take a deep breath and remember that attitude is a choice.

■ Decide whether you want to have a bad attitude or a good one.

■ Repeat to yourself that you are the source of your attitude.

■ Ask yourself, Who is in charge of your attitude—you or somebody outside of you?

# EXERCISE 14.6: SUPER SERVICE ACTION PLAN

The actions I will take as a result of this activity are:

1. _____

_____

_____

_____

2. _____

_____

_____

_____

3. _____

_____

_____

_____

4. _____

_____

_____

5. _____

_____

_____

6. _____

_____

_____

I will review this action plan on: _____      _____

                                            (date)                                (signed)

## Background and Purpose

Whether a customer service provider deals with large numbers of unknown customers each day and has no long-term relationship, or interacts with the same customers every day and knows them very well, preparation is key to having smooth interactions and good communication.

Without preparation, the interaction can go any way. The customer service provider has no control. This activity helps customer service providers understand the importance of preparing for a customer interaction and, more importantly, how to prepare.

## Objectives

By the end of this activity, participants will be able to:

1. Understand the importance of preparation.

2. Know how to prepare.

## Time

Approximately 1 hour 30 minutes

## Materials Required

1. Overhead 15.1

2. Flip chart and markers

3. Exercise 15.2

4. Exercise 15.3

## Mini Lecture

Every customer interaction seems different; however if you begin to examine them, you will notice that there are many similarities. This is the first step in preparation. What always or often happens in your interactions with customers? Do certain issues always come up? Do you notice that some problems never get resolved? Are there recurring bottlenecks?

## Activity 15

# Preparing for a Customer Interaction

We sometimes overwhelm our customers with too much information. Always think KISS: Keep It Simple and Sincere!

Preparing for customer interactions requires you to know what the customer expects and what you and your company have to offer. If you have ongoing relationships with certain key customers, you should keep a file that will help you to remember information about their business (especially if it is relevant to your own business).

The information you keep depends on your customer relationship. Some customer relationships can become quite personal, whereby the customer service provider knows the customer's hobbies, likes, and dislikes. It is important in this case to be honest. If a customer's hobby is skydiving and you are scared to death of airplanes, don't pretend to love air sports.

Preparation is knowing in advance what may come up. The more you can do to prepare for interactions, the better the outcome will be.

## Steps to Follow

1. Show Overhead 15.1. Ask the participants to share their experience of a customer service provider not being prepared. How did it make them feel?

2. Distribute Exercise 15.2. Ask each individual to complete the exercise and then ask for feedback and discussion.

3. Brainstorming exercise: Write the following heading at the top of a flip chart: Things We Should Know in Preparation.

4. Ask the participants to come up with as many things as possible that they should know about their customers before an interaction. You (or a designated scribbler) should make a list as the participants call them out.

5. Divide the participants into groups and give each group a list of things from the brainstorming session. (Each group should work on a different list. The length of the lists will depend on how many groups there are and how many things they came up with.)

6. Allow the groups 15 to 30 minutes to prepare a short overview of their lists: What are the most important things on the list? How would you prepare for them? What resources are available? Explain that they will each have 5 minutes to present their findings to the rest of the group.

7. Provide feedback after each group has presented.

8. Distribute Exercise 15.3.

9. Ask if anyone has questions. Provide a summary and wrap up.

# PREPARING FOR A CUSTOMER INTERACTION

1.   What is their business?

2.   How does it fit in with your company?

3.   If you have regular contact, be sincere about their interests.

4.   Expect objections and be prepared to handle them.

5.   Know the customer's past buying and service history: What products or services have they used? What (if anything) has changed?

## EXERCISE 15.2: CUSTOMER PREPARATION

Write the name of your customer: _____

What is your experience of this customer? _____

_____

_____

_____

Describe some typical problems you have experienced with this customer. _____

_____

_____

_____

What do you know about the customer that will help with future interactions? _____

_____

_____

_____

What can you do to prepare for future interactions? _____

_____

_____

_____

# EXERCISE 15.3: SUPER SERVICE ACTION PLAN

The actions I will take as a result of this activity are:

1. _____

   _____

   _____

   _____

2. _____

   _____

   _____

   _____

3. _____

   _____

   _____

   _____

4. _____

   _____

   _____

   _____

5. _____

   _____

   _____

   _____

6. _____

   _____

   _____

I will review this action plan on: _____    _____

                                      (date)                                     (signed)

# Maintaining a Positive Frame of Mind

What are the benefits of delivering Super Service from a customer service provider's point of view?

## Background and Purpose

Maintaining a positive frame of mind is one of the most important aspects of good business. It requires a "can-do" attitude even in the face of what might seem to be a failure.

Customer service does not work unless the people providing it have a positive frame of mind. It is the mind that provides solutions. The technology, product, or service are simply the tools.

## Objectives

By the end of this activity, participants will be able to:

1. Understand what having a positive frame of mind means to them.

2. Learn some tools for maintaining a positive frame of mind.

## Time

Approximately 1 hour 30 minutes

## Materials Required

1. Overheads 16.1, 16.2, 16.3, 16.5, and 16.6

2. Exercise 16.4 and Answers 16.4 B

3. Check-In Exercise 16.7

4. Exercise 16.8

## Mini Lecture

Having a positive frame of mind enables you to make decisions about what is right for you. It stops the chatter of negativity. There is a story about a group of people sitting at a sidewalk table having breakfast. An elderly man walked by and nodded toward the table, saying, "Are we all happy?"

The man was W. Clement Stone, one of the founders of Positive Mental Attitude; a millionaire many times over, this elderly man took the time to ask a bunch of strangers if they were happy. There was no reason for him to do it; no reason except that he makes the choice to be happy and it touches everyone around him.

You may think of yourself as a failure in life. You may look around and see other people who have an easier life than you. You might think that your job is harder, that you don't get paid enough, that customers are too demanding, you don't like the product or service your company sells, and you don't even like the people in your office very much. The reality is very different however. You have a job! You make the choice to enjoy it or not.

Let me share someone's life history with you.

This was a man who:

Failed at business at the age of 21.

Was defeated in a legislative race at age 23.

Failed again at business at age 24.

Overcame the death of his sweetheart at age 26.

Had a nervous breakdown at age 27.

Lost a congressional race at age 34.

Lost a congressional race at age 36.

Lost a senatorial race at age 45.

Failed in an effort to become vice president at age 47.

Lost a senatorial race at age 49.

Was elected president of the United States at age 52.

The man's name was Abraham Lincoln.

Thomas Edison tried 9,999 times to perfect the light bulb and hadn't succeeded. Someone asked him, "Are you going to have ten thousand failures?" He answered, "I didn't fail. I just discovered another way not to invent the electric light bulb."

## Steps to Follow

1. Show Overheads 16.1, 16.2, and 16.3. Discuss the possibility of choosing to have a positive frame of mind.

2. Hand out Exercise 16.4 and give participants 10 minutes to complete it.

3. Ask for feedback about the case study. Ask them how a shy person would act at a party: not talk, hang around the food, and so on. (Exercise 16.4 B has the answers.)

4. Show Overhead 16.5. Discuss the fact that our point of view creates the action that we take. The action that we take creates the results. Explain that our point of view is in the past. It creates action that we take in the present that creates results that happen in our future. If you think you are shy, you act like a shy person, which results in your being a shy person.

5. Show Overhead 16.6. Explain that the only way to maintain a Positive Mental Attitude is by making the choice to do it. Explain that even if you start out your day feeling great, the experience may wear off as the day draws to a close. This is the time to do it differently. You are responsible for being in control of the way you act and live your life.

6. Hand out Exercise 16.7 and ask participants to complete it.

7. Distribute Exercise 16.8 and ask participants to complete it.

8. Ask if there are any questions. Provide a brief summary and wrap up.

# Four Rules
# for a Positive Frame of Mind

1. Make yourself really important.

2. Respect yourself.

3. Respect your word.

4. Respect your agreements.

As long as you hold onto the belief that you don't matter,

that who you are does not count,

you can quit because,

after all,

"I am not important!"

You are!

You make the difference in the world!

# Beliefs act
# as anchors
# that keep
# us stuck.

## EXERCISE 16.4 A: CASE STUDY

Please read the following situations and answer the questions:

| Scene | Situation | Ending 1 | Ending 2 | Notes |
|---|---|---|---|---|
| 1. | A 61-year-old woman was told many years ago that her family is predisposed to heart problems. Her mother died at 61 and so did her grandfather. So she… | Worries about it for most of her life. Almost makes it to her sixty-second birthday, but dies two months earlier. | Determines not to worry about it, exercises, takes care of her weight, and takes life a whole lot less seriously than her parents ever did. | |
| 2. | An 8-year-old child is told by her math teacher that she is no good at math. So she… | Determines to study and learn math so she can show that the teacher is wrong. | Switches off in the math class because the child knows that math will always be an impossible subject to learn. | |
| 3. | A man goes to a party. He only knows two people there and they are actively engaged in conversation. He doesn't feel that he can interrupt. So he… | Goes to the food table and gets food, then finds a seat in the corner where he can eat and watch everyone else. | Mingles with the other people until he finds a conversation that he can join. | |

1. In scene 1, which ending makes a woman most in charge of her life?

   Please state why: _____

   _____

2. In scene 2, did the math teacher create the child's belief? _____

   Please state why: _____

3. In scene 3, which ending would a shy person take? _____

   Please state why: _____

   _____

# EXERCISE 16.4 B: CASE STUDY (ANSWERS)

| Scene | Situation | Ending 1 | Ending 2 | Notes |
|---|---|---|---|---|
| 1. | A 61-year-old woman was told many years ago that her family is predisposed to heart problems. Her mother died at 61 and so did her grandfather. So she… | Worries about it for most of her life. Almost makes it to her sixty-second birthday, but dies two months earlier. | Determines not to worry about it, exercises, takes care of her weight, and takes life a whole lot less seriously than her parents ever did. | Ending 1 makes the woman most in charge because she is taking responsibility for her life. |
| 2. | An 8-year-old child is told by her math teacher that she is no good at math. So she… | Determines to study and learn math so she can show that the teacher is wrong. | Switches off in the math class because the child knows that math will always be an impossible subject to learn. | The math teacher determined that the child was no good at math…when all along the child may only have needed extra help. |
| 3. | A man goes to a party. He only knows two people there and they are actively engaged in conversation. He doesn't feel that he can interrupt. So he… | Goes to the food table and gets food, then finds a seat in the corner where he can eat and watch everyone else. | Mingles with the other people until he finds a conversation that he can join. | The shy person would take ending 1 and hide behind the activity of getting and eating food. |

# BELIEFS CREATE OUR PERSONALITY

## POINT OF VIEW is in the PAST

### which creates

## ACTION which is in the PRESENT

### which creates

## RESULTS which are in the FUTURE

1. Prepare yourself for every event.

2. Think about your job and look for opportunities
to raise the standard.

3. Pay attention. Look for situations
where you can be your best.

4. Maintain a positive frame of mind
by finding ways to make a positive difference.

# EXERCISE 16.7: CHECK-IN

We learn by example, so choose one person who you believe has the right attitude. Complete the following questions.

1. What is it about this person that makes him or her so positive?

   • Is she more outgoing?

   • Does he smile more?

   • Is she giving?

   • Does he go with the flow?

   • Does she have fewer defenses?

   • Does he make an effort to go forward with a better attitude?

   • If anger comes up for her , does she get rid of it quickly?

   • If someone insults him, does he take it personally, or shrug it off?

Please write your answer here, especially if it is not one of the qualities listed above: _____

_____

_____


2. Choose one of the positive qualities that you most want to bring into your own life: _____

_____

# EXERCISE 16.8: SUPER SERVICE ACTION PLAN

The actions I will take as a result of this activity are:

1. _____
   _____
   _____
   _____

2. _____
   _____
   _____
   _____

3. _____
   _____
   _____
   _____

4. _____
   _____
   _____
   _____

5. _____
   _____
   _____
   _____

6. _____
   _____
   _____
   _____

I will review this action plan on: _____     _____
                                        (date)                              (signed)

## Activity 17

# Understand the Customer's Needs

Imagining what it is like to be your customer is a powerful customer service technique.

## Background and Purpose

Meeting needs is an important part of customer satisfaction. If we do not know what the customer needs, then how will we know how to satisfy those needs? This activity is short, simple, to the point, and very easy to understand.

## Objectives

By the end of this activity, participants will be able to:

1. Understand what a need is.

2. Help customers communicate their needs.

## Time

Approximately 1 hour

## Materials Required

1. Overhead 17.1

2. Exercise 17.2 and Answers 17.2 B

3. Exercise 17.3

## Mini Lecture

Other people's shoes rarely fit, so if we want to understand people better, we have to make allowances. Have you ever been told to "put yourself in someone else's position" or to "stand in their shoes"? What does it really mean?

Can we ever truly "see" something from another person's point of view? Can we ever know what it is like to lose a job, unless we have lost one ourselves? The answer must be no.

It is impossible to understand someone else's experience unless it has happened to us, and even then, it will be different. There is a way to communicate needs, however, and also to listen for them. That is what we will do in this activity.

## Steps to Follow

1. Show Overhead 17.1. Explain that the communication process is a two-way flow, back and forward from one person to another.

2. Divide the participants into pairs and give each pair a copy of Exercise 17.2. Ask them to read it and complete the questions together.

3. Use Exercise 17.2 B (Answers) to discuss the group's findings. (If you prefer, you can ask each pair to present their findings to the group.)

4. Distribute Exercise 17.3. Ask participants to complete it individually.

5. Ask if there are any questions. Provide a summary and wrap up by finding out what changes the participants will bring into the workplace as a result of this activity.

## Discussion Points

1. Ask the group if they have any experience of miscommunication.

2. Ask the group if they have ever given instructions to another person, and that person got them completely wrong.

3. Discuss the fact that if we give someone a job, we have to tell them what the finished job will look like. For example, "Jim, this is what a report looks like to me: table of contents, executive summary, content, and a final summary. Does this look like something you could do? When can you have it back to me?"

1.  A tells something to B.

2.  B listens and responds back to A.

3.  A listens and confirms,
    "Yes that's what I meant!" or denies,
    "No, that's not what I meant."

4.  A explains again.

5.  B listens and responds.

Eventually, the two reach agreement!

# EXERCISE 17.2: COMMUNICATING NEEDS

Please read the following two case studies and answer the questions below:

| Scene | Situation | Ending 1 | Ending 2 | Notes |
|---|---|---|---|---|
| 1. | A teenager goes into a music store and asks for a CD. The assistant has never heard of the group. So he… | Looks it up on the computer, sees it is not there, and tells the teenager, "Sorry, we don't have it!"<br><br>The teenager walks out. | Looks it up on the computer, sees it is not there, and asks the teenager a series of questions: "Is this a new group? Have you heard the CD? When do you need it for?" After a series of responses, the assistant understands where to get the CD. After one short phone call, he tells the teenager that he will have it in the store the following day.<br><br>Next day, the teenager comes into the store and buys the CD. | |
| 2. | A customer goes into a computer store and tells the assistant that she has $1,500 to spend on a computer system. The assistant takes a long time putting the system together. Meanwhile the customer is reading through the store catalog and sees exactly the system she wants. She asks for that one. The assistant replies… | "We don't have any of those left. That's one of our top sellers; they come in and go out practically the same day."<br><br>The customer replies, "I think I'll wait, thank you." The customer leaves the store. | "Absolutely. I can have one of those for you in about two weeks. Can you wait until then?"<br><br>The customer replies that she can and they complete the order.<br><br>"Great, all we need to do is fill out this paperwork and I will contact you as soon as it comes in." | |

1. In scene 1, what was the difference between endings 1 and 2? Please write the answer:

_____

_____

_____

2. In scene 2, how could ending 1 have ended better? _____

   What was the main difference between the two endings? _____

   _____


3. Have you ever experienced anything similar to the scenarios described? _____

   _____

   _____

# EXERCISE 17.2 B: COMMUNICATING NEEDS (ANSWERS)

| Scene | Situation | Ending 1 | Ending 2 | Notes |
|---|---|---|---|---|
| 1. | A teenager goes into a music store and asks for a CD. The assistant has never heard of the group. So he... | Looks it up on the computer, sees it is not there, and tells the teenager, "Sorry, we don't have it!"<br><br>The teenager walks out. | Looks it up on the computer, sees it is not there, and asks the teenager a series of questions: "Is this a new group? Have you heard the CD? When do you need it for?" After a series of responses, the assistant understands where to get the CD. After one short phone call, he tells the teenager that he will have it in the store the following day.<br><br>Next day, the teenager comes into the store and buys the CD. | The main difference is that the assistant wants to find the CD and therefore asks a series of questions that help him find it. |
| 2. | A customer goes into a computer store and tells the assistant that she has $1,500 to spend on a computer system. The assistant takes a long time putting the system together. Meanwhile the customer is reading through the store catalog and sees exactly the system she wants. She asks for that one. The assistant replies... | "We don't have any of those left. That's one of our top sellers; they come in and go out practically the same day."<br><br>The customer replies, "I think I'll wait, thank you." The customer leaves the store. | "Absolutely. I can have one of those for you in about two weeks. Can you wait until then?"<br><br>The customer replies that she can and they complete the order.<br><br>"Great, all we need to do is fill out this paperwork and I will contact you as soon as it comes in." | If the assistant had the customer's best interest at heart, he or she would have explained about the top-selling system in the first place.<br><br>The difference, between the two endings is that in ending 2, the assistant recovers credibility by immediately putting the customer's needs first. |

# EXERCISE 17.3: SUPER SERVICE ACTION PLAN

The actions I will take as a result of this activity are:

1. _____

2. _____

3. _____

4. _____

5. _____

6. _____

I will review this action plan on: _____     _____
                                        (date)                        (signed)

## Background and Purpose

An open mind is a mind that is open to new experiences and new ideas. It is the ability to look at all sides of a problem without any preconceived judgments or prejudices.

In the fast-changing corporate world, employees need to have open minds. This is true not only for problem solving, but also for interactions between people, whether those interactions are with internal or external customers.

This activity teaches participants how to listen with an open mind. It will provide them with tools to enhance their communication skills and personal interactions.

## Objectives

By the end of this activity, participants will be able to:

1. Understand the concept of an open mind.

2. Learn the benefits of listening with an open mind.

3. Know how to solve customer problems with an open mind.

## Time

Approximately 45 minutes to 1 hour

## Materials Required

1. Overhead 18.1

2. Role Play Scenario 18.2

3. Exercise 18.3

## Mini Lecture

What is an open mind? We use it to define people: "That person has a very open mind," or "That person has a very closed mind!" What does it really mean? Do you have an open mind? More importantly, is it a good thing to have?

## Activity 18
# How to Listen with an Open Mind

In the business world, the phone is like a screwdriver. It can open things and close things, and it can also screw things up.

An open mind is a mind that is open to new experiences and new ideas, like an empty vessel ready to be filled. If you can listen to a problem with an open mind, you will fill your mind with the problem. When your mind has completely grasped the problem, then you can begin to think of a solution.

Why is it so hard to do? It's because the mind finds it so difficult to remain empty, and so unwilling to be filled with another person's problem. It fills itself up with solutions, then, desperately wanting to pour itself out, our mind becomes like a flash flood and we overwhelm our listeners with solutions. Even if the solutions are correct, the person with the problem will not hear them, because he or she needs to talk about the problem first.

## Steps to Follow

1. Show Overhead 18.1. Explain that having an open mind takes concentration and a willingness to be open-minded. It requires staying focused and bringing the mind back into focus every time it drifts away.

2. Divide the group into pairs and hand out Role Play Scenario 18.2. Each pair will have an opportunity to play the part of speaker and listener. Each role play will take 3 minutes. After the first role play, partners will change roles.

   When each pair has played the role of speaker and listener, ask them to team up with one other pair. Each person will have one minute to relay the information heard from the partner.

3. If you have time, ask participants to pair up with a different partner and repeat the exercise, enabling them to take greater care with their listening.

4. Ask the participants to share their thoughts about the exercise. Provide feedback.

5. Hand out Exercise 18.3 and ask participants to complete it.

6. Give a summary and ask if there are any questions before wrapping up.

## Discussion Points

1. How difficult is it to retain an open mind?

2. What blocks us from having an open mind?

# How to Retain an Open Mind

- Focus on the person who is speaking.

- Concentrate on the words.

- See the person for the first time.

- Listen for the real problem.

- Even if you have heard it all before,
  it is still a problem for this person.

# ROLE PLAY SCENARIO 18.2

Speaker: During this role play, you will choose one topic of conversation from the list below. You will be given 3 minutes to tell the other person everything you know about this topic.

Speaker

_____

_____

_____

Listener: Your job is to listen and remember as many facts as you can.

Listener

_____

_____

_____

When you have finished, you will reverse roles. The speaker for the second role play should choose a different topic.

1. My last vacation.

2. Where I live.

3. My greatest interest, hobby, or sport.

4. My job.

5. My family.

# EXERCISE 18.3: SUPER SERVICE ACTION PLAN

The actions I will take as a result of this activity are:

1. _____
   _____
   _____
   _____

2. _____
   _____
   _____
   _____

3. _____
   _____
   _____

4. _____
   _____
   _____

5. _____
   _____
   _____

6. _____
   _____
   _____

I will review this action plan on: _____    _____
                                         (date)                              (signed)

## Background and Purpose

More and more companies are realizing that customers are the most important thing in their portfolio. Talking with customers effectively is a skill that employees can learn.

This activity will help everyone to talk with customers in a more friendly way.

## Objectives

By the end of this activity, participants will be able to:

1. Understand a technique for talking with customers.

2. Talk with customers more easily.

## Time

Approximately 20 minutes

## Materials Required

1. Overhead 19.1

2. Exercise 19.2

## Mini Lecture

Some people find it easy to talk with customers, and some find it very hard. Whichever category you fall into, one thing is certain: We all have people in our lives, and we all have to talk to them.

Everything begins with a thought. If we think we can't communicate easily, then guess what happens? We can't communicate easily. This visualization technique is one that you can use to enhance your communication skills. It only takes a few moments and you can use it before any interaction. The more you use it, the easier it will be to follow.

# Visualization Technique: Talking with Customers

Imagining what it is like to be your customer is a powerful customer service technique.

## Steps to Follow

1. Show Overhead 19.1. Explain that participants will all have an opportunity to experience this visualization technique.

2. Say to the group: "Before we start the visualization technique, let's clear our minds. Close your eyes. Take a deep breath in and fill your lungs. Release the breath. Center on your breathing. Calm it until it is peaceful. As you breathe out, release your tension."

3. Read through the steps on Overhead 19.1.

4. Ask the group for feedback. How did it feel? Who has done something like this before? Is it something they can use? How can they adapt it?

5. Hand out Exercise 19.2 and ask participants to complete it.

6. Provide a summary and ask for questions.

## Discussion Points

1. Who uses visualization techniques to help in situations?

2. Will anyone share their experience?

# Visualization Technique: Talking with Customers

1. Think of the conversation as a gentle flowing river.

2. You and your customer are in one boat; you are steering.

3. Your job is to help the boat stay free from obstructions.

4. You steer with gentle direction.

5. Your goal is to land safely and peacefully at the other end.

6. You never need to use force or waste energy.

7. If the river flows too quickly, you are still able to steer the boat to calmer waters.

8. You have the capability.

9. You have the strength.

10. You have the will.

# EXERCISE 19.2: SUPER SERVICE ACTION PLAN

The actions I will take as a result of this activity are:

1. _____

_____

_____

_____

2. _____

_____

_____

_____

3. _____

_____

_____

4. _____

_____

_____

5. _____

_____

_____

6. _____

_____

_____

I will review this action plan on: _____     _____
                                        (date)                              (signed)

## Activity 20

# How to Use Open and Closed Questions

## Background and Purpose

Open-ended questions are essential for getting specific details, because they help customers open up and respond with a wider range of information. However, it is very important to understand how and when to use open-ended questions, because using too many will sound like an interrogation.

This activity will help participants know how to use open and closed questions within the framework of customer communication.

## Objectives

By the end of this activity, participants will be able to:

1. Understand what an open question is.

2. Understand what a closed question is.

3. Understand when and how to use both types of questions with customers.

## Time

Approximately 1 hour

## Materials Required

1. Overheads 20.1, 20.2, and 20.3

2. Role Play Scenarios 20.4 A, B, C, and D.

3. Exercise 20.5

## Mini Lecture

Open-ended questions often begin with who, what, when, where, why, and how. Closed questions help the customer verify or confirm specific details or facts. It is good to use both open and closed questions. If too many closed questions are used, the customer can feel intimidated, frustrated, or irritated. Asking too many closed questions makes the customer feel that you are not really interested in his or her opinion.

Often we read about techniques like open and closed questions and think, "Ah yes, I know all about that." Then we wonder why we do not have all the information we need. It takes skill to use a technique, and all techniques need to be practiced.

To be a Super Service provider, you have to look at how you treat people in general. Do you go into an attack mode or a defend mode when you feel threatened or criticized? Do you interrupt people, or let them say what they feel? Do you take things personally? Are you too sensitive about what other people are saying and doing?

## Steps to Follow

1. Show Overhead 20.1. Explain that open-ended questions allow the customer to literally open up! The customer has no alternative but to respond with an answer that is more than a "yes" or "no." Emphasize that asking too many questions will sound like an interrogation.

2. Show Overhead 20.2. Explain that a closed-ended question stops the customer from continuing to talk too much. The customer has no alternative but to answer with "yes" or "no." Emphasize that using too many closed questions will make the conversation a series of "yes" and "no" answers, and that you may not get all the information you need.

3. Show Overhead 20.3. Suggest that the next time participants are with a customer, a friend, or a significant other, they practice the technique. Look into the person's eyes but do not stare! Focus attention on the speaker and when your mind wanders, bring it back. Watch body language for clues about how the other person is really feeling. People who are fidgeting, or scratching their heads may be uncomfortable about the conversation. Do the words mirror the body language? How can you make people feel more comfortable to express themselves? Do not take it personally! When you are angry or frustrated, it is always about you...not the other person. It is the same for your customers.

4. Have participants find a partner. Hand out Role Play Scenarios 20.4 A and B to each pair. Ask them to read the role play instructions (one should play the role of customer and one the role of customer service provider). Allow 5 minutes to role play each situation.

5. Hand out Role Play Scenarios 20.4 C and D. Have participants play the opposite roles. Give them 5 minutes to complete the role plays, then ask for feedback and facilitate a question-and-answer session.

6. Hand out Exercise 20.5 and ask participants to complete it.

7. Provide a summary and wrap up.

## Discussion Points

1. Do you notice when and how you use questions at this time?

2. Do you use more open or closed questions?

3. Have you noticed body language and matched it to what people are saying?

# Open-Ended Questions Are:

- "When did you first experience this problem?"

- "What was the effect of this?"

- "Who else is responsible for this decision?"

- "Why do you think this only occurs twice in the cycle?"

- "Where else has this type of problem occurred?"

- "How was this resolved last time?"

# Closed-Ended Questions Are:

■ "Does this happen every day?"

■ "Has this happened before?"

■ "Do you want them all to change?"

■ "Can we deliver tomorrow?"

■ "Is there anything else?"

■ "Will you monitor the outcome?"

# When asking questions:

- Look into the customer's eyes when he or she is talking to you (but do not stare the person down).

- Focus all your attention on the customer.

- Bring your mind back to focus if it wanders off.

- Pay attention to body language as well as words.

- Do the words mirror the body language?

- It is not a personal insult if a customer is angry.

# ROLE PLAY SCENARIO 20.4 A
# OPEN AND CLOSED QUESTIONS–SCENARIO ONE

## CUSTOMER SERVICE REPRESENTATIVE

**Scenario One:** You are a customer service representative. The caller is a very distraught homeowner whose stove is not working and who needs it by this evening. It is now 11 a.m. Your job is to ask a series of open and closed questions to understand the problem and find a solution.

CUSTOMER

**Scenario One:** You are the customer. Your stove is not working. A repair person came at 9 a.m. and tried to mend it, but had the wrong part. The repair person said she was running late, and did not think she could get back to you today. You call customer service to complain.

# ROLE PLAY SCENARIO 20.4 C
# OPEN AND CLOSED QUESTIONS–SCENARIO TWO

## CUSTOMER SERVICE REPRESENTATIVE

**Scenario Two:** You are a customer service representative. The caller is a very distraught homeowner. She is saying that she has a one-year Scotch Guard warranty for her sofa. She does not have the paperwork, but is sure it still applies. You recently got burned by a customer when you set him up to have his sofa cleaned after his warranty had run out.

## CUSTOMER

**Scenario Two:** You are the customer. Your sofa has a Scotch Guard warranty that is about to run out. You are sure about this because you bought the sofa the first week in September of last year, and now it is the last week in August. You cannot find the receipt, but you paid by store credit card. You want someone to come tomorrow to clean the sofa. You are throwing a very important party for your boss.

# EXERCISE 20.5: SUPER SERVICE ACTION PLAN

The actions I will take as a result of this activity are:

1. _____
   _____
   _____
   _____

2. _____
   _____
   _____
   _____

3. _____
   _____
   _____
   _____

4. _____
   _____
   _____
   _____

5. _____
   _____
   _____
   _____

6. _____
   _____
   _____

I will review this action plan on: _____     _____
                                              (date)                                (signed)

## Background and Purpose

Every customer has a need—but how does a company know that its employees understand the customer's needs? The answer is through customer service providers who verify and clarify needs.

## Objectives

By the end of this activity, participants will be able to:

1. Listen for what the customer really needs, wants, or desires.

2. Check whether the customer's needs have been answered.

## Time

Approximately 45 minutes

## Materials Required

1. Overheads 21.1 and 21.2

2. Role Play Scenario 21.3, 21.3 B, 21.4, 21.4 B

3. Exercise 21.5

## Mini Lecture

Unless your mind is open to needs, you will never know whether you are doing a good job or not. You may provide the technical solution, but you may not have answered the customer's need or desire.

One way to check whether you have answered your customer's needs is to clarify facts. This means restating details, such as numbers, spelling of names and addresses, quantities, time lines, dates, delivery needs, and so on.

# Activity 21
# Verify and Clarify Needs

We sometimes overwhelm our customers with too much information. Always think KISS: Keep It Simple and Sincere!

## Steps to Follow

1. Show Overhead 21.1. Explain that these are examples of verifying needs.

2. Show Overhead 21.2. Explain that one way to ensure you have understood the customer's needs is to repeat them back to him or her.

3. Divide the class into pairs. Hand out Role Play Scenario 21.3 and 21.3 B. Ask pairs to take turns playing speaker and listener. Allow participants 5 minutes to role play a scenario; then have them change roles. Give them Role Play Scenarios 21.4 and 21.4 B. Allow another 5 minutes.

4. Debrief the exercise. If you have time, ask participants to switch partners and repeat the exercise, using a different topic.

5. Hand out Exercise 21.5 and ask participants to complete it.

6. Provide a summary. Ask if there are any questions and wrap up.

## Discussion Points

1. What situations are most confusing in a customer service setting?

2. How will this activity help you provide clarity in customer service interactions?

## Verify and Clarify Needs

- "I understand there were 15 parts delivered
  and you need 25. Is that correct?"

- "Let me see if I understand.
  You paid the bill on July 2nd,
  and your last statement did not reflect that?"

- "So what you are saying, Jane,
  is that when the thermostat is on high,
  the furnace blows out cold air.
  Have I got that right?"

# Restate Your Understanding of the Problem

*"Am I correct in thinking that you want a new thermostat?"*

Unless you paraphrase your understanding of the problem and the solution, you and your customer may be on different wavelengths.

# ROLE PLAY SCENARIO 21.3

**Listener:** Your job is to verify the customer's needs. What are the customer's needs and what does the customer want to do about the problem? This is not the same as finding a solution. When you have the problem verified, then you can find a solution.

_____

_____

_____

# ROLE PLAY SCENARIO 21.3 B

**Speaker:** Please begin the scenario with one of the sentences here:

1. I am returning this bucket because it's no good. It doesn't fit the work I do as a painter. The brushes don't fit. The plastic is too stiff. The handle is too big.

2. The tree I bought here last week has died. I watered it and the leaves started to drop off. All the other trees I bought are fine; it's just this one that died. I don't really like it anyway; the flowers aren't the same as on the other trees.

**ROLE PLAY SCENARIO 21.4**

**Listener:** Your job is to verify the customer's needs. What are the customer's needs and what does the customer want to do about the problem? This is not the same as finding a solution. When you have the problem verified, then you can find a solution.

_____

_____

_____

# ROLE PLAY SCENARIO 21.4 B

**Speaker:** Please begin the scenario with one of the sentences here:

1. We filled the bathtub with water as directed, turned on the whirlpool, and water sprayed all over the bathroom. It doesn't work.

2. I ordered 60 parts and only 30 came. It's never happened before with you, but I don't know if I can rely on you any more.

# EXERCISE 21.5: SUPER SERVICE ACTION PLAN

The actions I will take as a result of this activity are:

1. _____

_____

_____

_____

2. _____

_____

_____

_____

3. _____

_____

_____

4. _____

_____

_____

5. _____

_____

_____

6. _____

_____

_____

I will review this action plan on: _____        _____
                                          (date)                              (signed)

## Activity 22

# Barriers That Inhibit Problem Solving

You can foresee stress.
You can foresee burnout.
You can plan how to handle them.

## Background and Purpose

Every organization has problems. Every customer service provider has to deal with problems. The only way to deal with a problem effectively is to look at it in a different light.

This activity is designed to show participants how to look at problems differently. It will teach the participants that a problem is something that allows us to move forward. Problems keep the organization from getting stuck. Problems can be energizers and innovators.

## Objectives

By the end of this activity, participants will be able to:

1. Look at problems differently.

2. Understand that a problem is something that will move them forward.

3. Know how to deal with problems effectively.

## Time

Approximately 2 hours

## Materials Required

1. Overheads 22.1, 22.2, 22.3, 22.4, 22.5, and 22.6

2. Exercises 22.7 and 22.8

## Mini Lecture

If we need problems to move us forward, why do we dislike them so much? One of the reasons is because they do move us forward! Sometimes we like to feel comfortable: to stay in the same place, to not have to think or move. What happens, however, is that we do move anyway. We are not trees; we cannot stay in the same spot. Problems are a part of life, so we may as well embrace them and allow them to move us forward.

## Steps to Follow

1. Show Overhead 22.1. Explain the definition of the word *problem*. Make sure the participants understand that a problem moves us forward. Every invention was made because there was a problem doing something the old way, and a new way needed to be found.

2. Show Overhead 22.2. Explain that if you are too busy with your own problems to help your customer, the problem (and the customer) will not be resolved. They will simply go somewhere else, and then you lose control of the solution.

3. Show Overhead 22.3. Explain that you must keep your mind focused on the goal, which is to help solve the customer's problem. This will keep you unaffected by the customer's attitude. It will help you remain objective and not take things personally. Remember, to the customer, you represent your company. You could be a saint, but the customer will distrust you if that is what is in his or her mind.

4. Show Overhead 22.4. Everyone has a customer, and everyone is a customer. To make this idea a reality, we must always think, "How will this decision affect my customer?" It has to do with relationships between departments, not just within them. If we can create a dynamic sense of teamwork and camaraderie, it not only makes the company thrive, but we benefit as individuals also.

5. Show Overhead 22.5. Another barrier to solving problems is not taking responsibility. It's important that customers know you are sincere in wanting to help them, that you don't just want to provide a solution (any solution), and that you want to correctly diagnose the problem.

6. Show Overhead 22.6. If the problem seems to be one of distrust or lack of ability, look for some common ground. This means acknowledging that the problem is valid and that you want to work together with the customer. "I can understand why you are frustrated with the inconsistency; let's work together to find the root cause of the problem."

7. Hand out Exercise 22.7. Group participants into teams of four. Have them read the exercise notes. Then ask each of the team members to come up with a typical communication problem (with either internal or external customers). Ask them to review each problem and brainstorm a phrase that would help to overcome the problem. Explain that each team will have 5 to 10 minutes to present problems and phrases that will help. Allow 5 minutes of individual brainstorming to start, and let participants know how much time they have left.

8. Allow each team to present its findings.

9. Ask for feedback. Discuss the exercise.

10. Hand out Exercise 22.8 and ask participants to complete it individually.

11. Provide a summary and wrap up.

# Definition of the Word *Problem*

- *Problem* comes from the root word *problema*: to lay before or to throw.

- Problems move us forward.

# Problems Do Not Go Away

If you do not help your customers to solve their problems,

- They will take their problems somewhere else.

- You have pushed your responsibility onto someone else.

- You have lost control of the customers.

- You lose credibility with your coworkers.

- Your customers lose faith in you.

# The Customer's Attitude Can Be a
# Barrier to Solving Problems

The customer

■ Does not want to work with you.

■ Wants to work against you.

■ Does not trust you.

■ Does not respect your ability to help.

# YOU MUST KEEP FOCUSED ON THE GOAL: TO HELP SOLVE THE PROBLEM

# If the customer has difficulty explaining the problem, you will hear phrases such as:

- "It's very confusing…"

- "I just can't figure it out!"

- "I'm not sure how to…"

- "It doesn't seem to…"

**Be patient. Remember, you know all about your product or service, but your customer may not. Here are some tips:**

1. Speak slowly.

2. Use short sentences.

3. Be tactful.

4. Ask, "Do you have any questions?" or, "Am I being clear?"

# EXERCISE 22.7: PHRASES THAT HELP

Here is an example of phrases that help in problem-solving situations.

"I can understand that being without your product will result in lost business, and I like your idea about trading it in for a new one. Let's run with that idea. We'll give you a new one for a small loaner fee while yours is being fixed. This way, you can try out the features of one of our new models; how does that sound?"

"I think that's a great idea. We'll repair your van after you've finished your work for the day, and you can pick it up the next morning. That way you won't lose any business."

Write in the space below a typical or ongoing communication problem that you have (with either an internal or external customer).

_____

_____

_____

_____

_____

With the help of your team, write down a phrase that will help solve this communication problem.

_____

_____

_____

_____

_____

**Be prepared to present your answer to the rest of the group.**

# EXERCISE 22.8: SUPER SERVICE ACTION PLAN

The actions I will take as a result of this activity are:

1.  _____
    _____
    _____
    _____

2.  _____
    _____
    _____
    _____

3.  _____
    _____
    _____
    _____

4.  _____
    _____
    _____

5.  _____
    _____
    _____

6.  _____
    _____
    _____

I will review this action plan on: _____      _____
                                     (date)                             (signed)

# Activity 23

# Honesty as a Tool

## Background and Purpose

Honesty and integrity are highly valued in most organizations. Using honesty as a tool provides an advantage that outweighs most others. It not only helps with trust issues between employees, but it engenders trust with your customers also.

This activity talks about honesty as a tool and using it as a skill that can be learned. If a company does not show its employees the value of being honest, it may lose its customers.

## Objectives

By the end of this activity, participants will be able to:

1. Understand the meaning of honesty.

2. Understand that honesty is a tool and using it is a skill that can be learned.

## Time

Approximately 45 minutes

## Materials Required

1. Overheads 23.1 and 23.2

2. Role Play Scenario 23.3

3. Exercise 23.4

## Mini Lecture

Everything you are inside is reflected in the way you treat people. It is almost impossible to think gentle thoughts and act with anger at the same time. Alternatively, it is very difficult to think angry thoughts and act with peace.

If your product or service has created a problem for your customer, you must acknowledge that. If a customer is very unhappy about the problem, you must help to find a solution. Customers have more faith in a company that is big enough to say, "Yes, we made a mistake, and we have enough strength and power behind us to correct it!"

You are your own company. If your boss wants you to lie to customers, it is not the company that is having to lie—it is you! You make the ultimate decision. You do not have to walk out of your job and lose your earnings, but you do have choices. You can move to another department or report the matter. You are writer, director, producer, and star player in your life. You make the choice to stay with the script or change it. The only thing you can never change is your customer.

## Steps to Follow

1. Show Overhead 23.1. It's easy to think that I will be honest now and then say things that could be very hurtful to the other person. Using honesty is not an excuse to dump everything you have wanted to say but never had the courage to say onto another person. Before you are honest, ask yourself, "Is it kind; is it necessary; is it wise?"

2. Show Overhead 23.2, about how to dialogue honesty with other people. Notice that the language allows for a dialogue. You don't just state your point of view; you say how you feel or see the situation, and ask for the other person's perspective.

3. Hand out Role Play Scenario 23.3. Ask participants to pair up and read the handout. You can facilitate this role play by interacting with pairs if they are struggling. Notice whether there is a lack of seeing the other person's point of view. The goal in this exercise is for each person to be honest about his or her perspective, while listening to and accepting the other person's perspective, which is different. Allow 5 to 10 minutes for this role play.

   *Trainer tips for the role play:* If people are struggling with explaining their perspective, they can describe what their color feels like. For example, blue is peaceful and cool; it often symbolizes water. Red is hot and angry and often symbolizes fire.

4. Ask for feedback after the role play. Discuss what worked and what did not work with the group.

5. Hand out Exercise 23.4. Ask participants to complete it and then discuss how they feel about the exercise.

6. Provide a summary and answer any questions before wrapping up.

## Insights to Look For

1. Ask if participants can see how honesty would work in their situation.

2. Ask if participants have been in a situation in which honesty did or did not work.

# Honesty as a Tool

1. **Think kind thoughts.**
   **"Is it kind?"**

2. **Speak gently.**
   **"Is it necessary?"**

3. **Use wisdom.**
   **"Is it wise?"**

# Honesty as a Tool

■ "I have a concern, and I would like to share my thoughts about it with you and then ask for your reaction."

■ "It looks different from my perspective; please tell me what you have seen or heard that leads you to see it that way."

■ "Making an informed decision is more important to me than being right or winning; so I would like to hear your point of view, especially if it differs from my own."

# ROLE PLAY SCENARIO 23.3: HONESTY AS A SKILL

The issue: Imagine you are both sitting in a room and you cannot move from your seats. There is a ball hanging from the ceiling. One side of the ball is colored blue. The other side is colored red.

Blue Person: Your role is to be honest. You see the ball as blue. Your job is to make the other person understand that the ball is blue.

Red Person: Your role is to be honest. You see the ball as red. Your job is to make the other person understand that the ball is red.

Both parties will explain their positions *without arguing,* and still keep the integrity of their colors.

Some questions that will help the dialogue are:

■ "Could you help me understand how you came to that conclusion?"

■ "Can you give me an example of what you mean?"

■ "Can you help me understand why you think this is so?"

■ "Could there be an alternative explanation other than the one you just gave?"

## EXERCISE 23.4: SUPER SERVICE ACTION PLAN

The actions I will take as a result of this activity are:

1. _____

   _____

   _____

   _____

2. _____

   _____

   _____

   _____

3. _____

   _____

   _____

   _____

4. _____

   _____

   _____

5. _____

   _____

   _____

6. _____

   _____

   _____

I will review this action plan on: _____     _____
                                          (date)                              (signed)

## Activity 24

# Work Together

## Background and Purpose

Every company is made up of people. Its goal maybe to sell products or services, but without people these goals will never be fulfilled. One of the key elements to a successful company is having the people work together. If the people are not working together, the company will be unable to meet the needs of its customers.

This activity highlights the importance of working together. It uses two improvisation techniques to communicate how to work together.

## Objectives

By the end of this activity, participants will be able to:

1. Understand the importance of working together.

2. Use a communication tool called "Yes and... ."

3. Use a communication tool called "Discover, explore, and heighten."

## Time

Approximately 1 hour

## Materials Required

1. Overhead 24.1

2. Role Play Scenario 24.2

3. Exercises 24.3 and 24.4

## Mini Lecture

One of the main reasons people do not work together is fear. Our fears can be huge or small, but as long as we have them, we build walls. Walls do not create an atmosphere of working together.

This was well-stated by a *New York Times* reporter: "The difference between people who work in corporations and news reporters is that reporters work in isolation and look for adversity, whereas corporate people work in teams and look for commonality."

Commonality does not mean a lack of creativity or that everyone gets blended together; it simply means being able to state a point of view without getting "blasted out of the water!" It means using dialogue and being in communication.

One of the biggest stumbling blocks in working together is when someone keeps saying, "No." When one person is putting forward a point of view and the other person says "No," the conversation will soon die out or come into conflict. Today, we will learn how to work together by using two simple improvisation exercises. One is called "Yes, and… ." The other is called "Discover, explore, and heighten."

## Steps to Follow

1. Show Overhead 24.1 Explain that "Yes, and..." is an improvisation technique used by actors to keep a flow of communication going. It is designed to prevent "blocks" being put up between two people.

2. Have participants find a partner and hand each pair the Role Play Scenario 24.2. Ask participants to read the activity and start the role play. Allow 5 to 10 minutes.

3. Hand out Exercise 24.3. Ask the participants to form groups of 3 or 4 depending on the total number of people. Ask them to begin the activity. Stress that they should still use "Yes and… ."

   Debrief this exercise by asking the participants how they felt.

4. Hand out Exercise 24.4 and ask participants to complete it and give feedback on their answers.

5. Provide a brief summary and answer any questions before wrapping up.

## Discussion Points

1. Can "Yes, and..." be used in an angry way?

   The answer is yes. If the tone of voice does not reflect a willingness to communicate, it will come off as angry.

2. Can "Yes, and..." be used too often?

   The answer is yes. If it is used as a response every time, it will lose it's meaning, which is to make the conversation flow.

3. What is valuable about the exercise, "Discover, explore, and heighten"?

   One of the answers may be that we often look ahead so much that we forget to examine what's happening right now.

   Another answer is that some solutions are so obvious we overlook them—we can only see clearly when we 'look closely' at everything.

# "YES, AND..."

# ROLE PLAY SCENARIO 24.2

Each person in the role play will choose a topic from this list:

- My favorite sport

- My favorite food

- My best vacation

- The most meaningful day in my life

- Why I love my car

- What I enjoy most on the weekends

Without telling the other person your choice, both of you begin to have a conversation. Your job is to show interest in what the other person is saying and to build on the other person's point by using "Yes, and..." *while at the same time* steering the conversation back to your topic!

## EXERCISE 24.3: DISCOVER, EXPLORE, AND HEIGHTEN

Please read the following scenario carefully.

This is a game about moving an event forward. Someone discovers something and everyone's job is to explore and heighten the discovery. For example, a scene may sound like this:

John:    "Wow, look at this fossil I've found. It must be a million years old!"

Mary:    "Yes, and it reminds me of the one we found yesterday in that cave."

Hank:    "Yes, and look at these markings on it. I think it was carved into a tool."

You and your team will play the following activity. Your job is to discover, explore, and heighten as a team.

You are in a desert searching for a spaceship that was reported lost in the vicinity over 200 years ago. Everything that you need will materialize in your hands like magic: tools, equipment, maps, etc. Anything that you wish to happen will happen. For example, if you find a piece of metal or glass, all you have to say is, "Look at this piece of metal!" and everyone else will see it.

Some important rules to remember: You are not allowed to deny another player. In other words, if someone says, "Look at this unusual rock!" your job is to explore it with them and say something like, "Wow, it looks as if it was heated to a very high temperature at one time!"

# EXERCISE 24.4: SUPER SERVICE ACTION PLAN

The actions I will take as a result of this activity are:

1. _____
   _____
   _____
   _____

2. _____
   _____
   _____
   _____

3. _____
   _____
   _____

4. _____
   _____
   _____

5. _____
   _____
   _____

6. _____
   _____
   _____

I will review this action plan on: _____     _____
                                        (date)                              (signed)

## Activity 25

# How to Give Information

## Background and Purpose

Information is power. When you have information, you have power. Unfortunately, many people abuse that power. They give too much of it away at inappropriate times. We may tell customers too much about the product or service, causing information overload.

The purpose of the activity is to teach how to give information: the right amount at the right time. If people understand how to do this, they will have better relations with customers, increase customer satisfaction, and ultimately increase sales.

## Objectives

By the end of this activity, participants will be able to:

1. Understand basic rules about giving information.

2. Know the difference between redundant language and useful language.

## Time

Approximately 45 minutes

## Materials Required

1. Overheads 25.1, 25.2, and 25.3

2. Exercises 25.4 and 25.5

## Mini Lecture

When we have information, we have the ball in our court; we have the information and we have the power. Our customers are like sponges at the other side of the court; if we are not careful we can drown them with information.

Maybe we don't normally get much air time in daily conversations; or we know our product or service inside out and want to tell someone all about it; or we think it's being honest to tell everything we know; or we just want to dominate the conversation. If you fall into any of these categories, stop for a moment and think!

Have you ever been bombarded with too much information? You're in a store and you know nothing about the product you want to buy. You ask for some information and the salesperson turns into a robot. After the first sentence, you stand there listening to all the jargon and you have no idea what the salesperson is talking about. You daren't even ask a question because you are so afraid the person will really answer it!

When we give information, we come from a powerful position. Depending on our skill and wisdom, we can enlighten customers or plunge them into darkness. We have the power to make our customers feel good or bad, just by the way we give information.

## Steps to Follow

1. Show Overhead 25.1. Explain that there are a few rules about giving information. Walk through the rules with them.

2. Show Overhead 25.2. Explain that there are also words and phrases that should be avoided when giving information.

3. Show Overhead 25.3. Explain that we often use too many words when one simple word is easier to understand.

4. Hand out Exercise 25.4. Here are the answers to the questions (point out the shortened phrases in bold).

   a. **We recommended** plan 100 to the board and should hear back next week.

   b. **We discussed** blowers and dryers with your customer and will go ahead soon.

   c. **We inspected** the plant and it needs much repair work.

   d. **We studied** the trees and the project is worthwhile.

5. Hand out Exercise 25.5. Ask participants to complete the exercise and then discuss their findings.

6. Summarize what they have learned and answer any questions.

## Discussion Points

1. What are the advantages of keeping our words simple?

2. What are some ways of doing this? (Answers include editing our written words.)

1. Be clear: *Use simple words without any jargon.*

2. Stick to the point: *Keep focused on the problem and solution.*

3. Be honest: *Do not overpromise and underperform.*

**"I'll be honest with you."**
*This sounds like everything you've
said up to that point was not honest!*

**"I can't."**
*This is like putting a brick wall
between you and your customer.
State what you can do, rather than what you
cannot do.*

**"I'll let you know."**
*When? Give a date and a time.
Make it happen!*

| Redundant | Use Instead |
|---|---|
| Assemble together | Assemble |
| General consensus of opinion | Consensus |
| Red in color | Red |
| Basic fundamentals | Fundamentals |
| Important essentials | Essentials |
| Due to the fact that | Because |
| In the event that | If |
| I am in receipt of | I received |

# EXERCISE 25.4

Please shorten the following sentences:

a. We finally made a recommendation to the board about plan 100, and we should hear back from them by the end of next week by the very latest.

_____

_____

b. We entered into a discussion with your customer about the blowers and dryers, and we may get the go-ahead very soon.

_____

_____

c. We made an inspection of the plant and have found it needs a very lot of repair work doing!

_____

_____

d. We performed a study of the trees and I am very pleased to announce that the project is definitely worthwhile doing.

_____

_____

# EXERCISE 25.5: SUPER SERVICE ACTION PLAN

The actions I will take as a result of this activity are:

1. _____

   _____

   _____

   _____

2. _____

   _____

   _____

   _____

3. _____

   _____

   _____

4. _____

   _____

   _____

5. _____

   _____

   _____

6. _____

   _____

   _____

I will review this action plan on: _____     _____
　　　　　　　　　　　　　　　　　　　　(date)　　　　　　　　　　　　　　　　　　(signed)

## Activity 26

# Product Profile from a Customer Perspective

Imagining what it is like to be your customer
is a powerful customer service technique.

## Background and Purpose

Most companies have their own terminology or jargon; mostly it is very confusing for customers. The T11 (substitute your own company jargon here) that you are so comfortable talking about with colleagues is confusing to new customers. Worse than that, it can make them feel really stupid if they have to keep asking, "What is that?"

The purpose of this activity is to create a product profile that the customer will understand.

## Objectives

By the end of this activity, participants will be able to:

1. Explain their products from a customer's perspective.

2. Understand why a product is successful.

## Time

Approximately 45 minutes

## Materials Required

1. Overheads 26.1 and 26.2

2. Exercises 26.3 and 26.4

## Mini Lecture

Whether your job entails explaining a product or a service to your customer, this exercise will help you understand your customers' needs better. It will help you learn to use words that are easy to say and listen to and avoid using jargon.

## Steps to Follow

1. Show Overhead 26.1 and explain the importance of not using jargon when talking with a customer.

2. Show Overhead 26.2. Ask participants to get into teams of 3 or 4 to discuss how their product or service works, what its benefits are to the customer, how it solves problems, and any other relevant information.

3. Hand out Exercise 26.3 and ask participants to complete it individually.

4. Debrief the session by asking individuals to share their thoughts about jargon, benefits, and product solutions.

5. Hand out Exercise 26.4 and ask participants to complete it.

6. Provide a summary of the session and answer any questions before wrapping up.

# Talking about Your Product or Service

1. **Choose the most familiar words.** If you shouted, "Quick, there's a conflagration!" many people would not know what to do. Best to shout "Fire!" instead.

2. **Eliminate jargon.** Take out any words that look strange.

3. **Build a foundation of key words.** In school you had to be creative and say the same thing in a different way each time. The business world is different, we need to be direct.

4. **Trim your sentences.** A long sentence is like nonstop talk. Chop the sentences to 15 or 18 words each.

# Product or Service Profile

- My product or service is called _ _ _ _ _ _

- It works by _ _ _ _ _ _

- Its benefits are _ _ _ _ _ _

- It solves problems by _ _ _ _ _ _

- Other information to add is _ _ _ _ _ _ _

# EXERCISE 26.3: PRODUCT OR SERVICE PROFILE

Write down your explanation of how your product or service operates:

My product or service is called _____

_____

It works by _____

_____

_____

Its benefits are _____

_____

_____

It solves problems by _____

_____

_____

Other information to add is _____

_____

_____

# EXERCISE 26.4: SUPER SERVICE ACTION PLAN

The actions I will take as a result of this activity are:

1. _____

_____

_____

_____

2. _____

_____

_____

_____

3. _____

_____

_____

_____

4. _____

_____

_____

5. _____

_____

_____

6. _____

_____

_____

I will review this action plan on: _____     _____
                                          (date)                            (signed)

## Background and Purpose

Every person in a customer service position has to give unwelcome information at some time or another. Because it is uncomfortable to give unwelcome information, people try to get it over with as fast as possible, sometimes too abruptly, which can damage the customer relationship even further.

This activity teaches how to give unwelcome information in an easier way.

## Objectives

By the end of this activity, participants will be able to:

1. Understand which words to use.

2. Use the good news—bad news approach.

## Time

Approximately 20 minutes

## Materials Required

1. Overheads 27.1, 27.2, and 27.3

2. Role Play Scenarios 27.4 A, 27.4 B, 27.5 A, and 27.5 B

3. Exercise 27.6

## Mini Lecture

If you are in customer service, there are times when you must give unwelcome news to your customer. That can be uncomfortable and we want to do it as fast as possible. This can sometimes create problems. The customer senses that we want to get it out of the way and move on, and this can make the customer feel unimportant.

The key to giving unwelcome news is to remain detached from the outcome. Give the bad news, and then get out of the way. This does not mean physically removing yourself; it means detaching

---

# Activity 27

# How to Give Unwelcome Information

yourself from the customer's emotions. If the customer is angry about the news, do not take it personally.

## Steps to Follow

1. Show Overhead 27.1. Ask, "Which of the sentences sounds like the speaker likes the raincoat?" The answer is, the bottom one! When we use the word *but* we are eliminating anything good we have said. "This raincoat keeps the water out, but..." means that we don't like the raincoat, even if it does keep the water out. "This raincoat keeps the water out, and..." means that not only does it keep the water out, it is also short, which is a good thing! When you use the word *but*, notice what you are really saying.

2. Show Overhead 27.2 and explain that we do not want to say to our customers, "Do you want the good news first, or the bad news?" However, including any good news with the bad news can help in some cases.

3. Show Overhead 27.3 and explain that it is important to encourage customers to participate in finding the right solution. When the customer is involved in finding the right solution, he or she is more likely to want the solution to work.

4. Ask everyone to find a partner for the role plays. Hand out Role Play Scenarios 27.4 A and 27.4 B to each pair. Ask them to begin.

5. After 5 minutes, ask them to change roles and hand each pair Role Play Scenarios 27.5 A and 27.5 B.

6. Ask for feedback about the role plays. How did the participants feel? What did they learn? What will they do differently as a result of the role plays?

7. Hand out Exercise 27.6 and ask participants to complete it.

8. Provide a short summary and answer any questions before wrapping up.

# The Meaning of the Word "But"

**"The raincoat keeps the water out, but it's short."**

**"The raincoat keeps the water out, and it's short."**

# Good News—Bad News

"To help your situation,
I have brought the installation
forward by two days.
However, I apologize
for the mistake with the
delivery charge.
The correct price is $75.00
instead of $60.00.
I am sorry for the error
and the inconvenience."

# Seek to Express, Not Impress

## "You mentioned an alternative solution earlier. What did you have in mind?"

### or,

## "That's an interesting way of dealing with this situation. Can you tell me more about it?"

# ROLE PLAY SCENARIO 27.4 A (CUSTOMER)

You will play the customer.

1. You have a television with a built-in VCR in your training room. You wanted to record a program that morning and the VCR has not worked.

2. You want the service person to come out now because there is another important program to record at 3 p.m. that same afternoon.

3. The reason for the urgency is that your boss is away and has asked that you record these programs. You want to do a good job.

# ROLE PLAY SCENARIO 27.4 B (SERVICE PROVIDER)

You will play the role of service provider.

1. You work for a company that makes televisions and VCRs.

2. Your job as a customer service provider is to dispatch repair staff to customer locations.

3. You are short on staff. You do have one repair person on stand-by to handle emergencies. However, there is an extra service charge for this use.

# ROLE PLAY SCENARIO 27.5 A  (CUSTOMER)

You will play the customer.

1. You are in charge of ordering office furniture for your boss. The chair you ordered does not swivel as it should.

2. Your boss complained to you about it at the beginning of the week, before going away. You forgot to do anything about it and the boss is coming back tomorrow.

3. You feel very stressed. You need to get the chair either repaired or replaced by tomorrow. You have called the company and have so far talked with two people in customer service. Both have been unable to help.

# ROLE PLAY SCENARIO 27.5 B (SERVICE PROVIDER)

You will play the role of service provider.

1.  You work for a company that makes office furniture. You handle difficult problems and customers. You have a small separate budget to solve really difficult problems.

2.  You are the one to decide whether a problem needs your special attention or not.

3.  Many times, problems come to you that do not warrant your attention.

# EXERCISE 27.6: SUPER SERVICE ACTION PLAN

The actions I will take as a result of this activity are:

1. _____

_____

_____

_____

2. _____

_____

_____

_____

3. _____

_____

_____

4. _____

_____

_____

5. _____

_____

_____

6. _____

_____

_____

I will review this action plan on: _____    _____
                                         (date)                                    (signed)

## Background and Purpose

The most important person to a customer is himself or herself. This activity focuses on how to make customers feel they are the most important people to the customer service provider and to the company.

## Objectives

By the end of this activity, participants will be able to:

1. Understand the importance of acknowledging a customer's feelings.

2. Know the words to use to acknowledge a customer's feelings.

## Time

Approximately 20 minutes

## Materials Required

1. Overhead 28.1

2. Flip chart

3. Exercise 28.2

# Activity 28

# Acknowledge the Customer's Feelings

## Mini Lecture

Who is the most important person to you? If you are honest, most of you will answer that you are! It is the same with customers. The most important people to your customers are themselves...certainly not you or your company. This activity focuses on how to make customers feel they are the most important people to you and to your company—and they are for the short time they are with you. If the customer is not important to you or the company, then you should not be in customer service!

184

## Steps to Follow

1. Show Overhead 28.1. Explain that when we acknowledge customers' feelings, it does not mean that we have to take their frustration on board. It just means that we sincerely understand how they feel. Remember how you feel when you buy something and it does not work. It is frustrating! If the customer service provider acknowledges the problem, it makes you feel much better. Ask the participants if they have a recent memory of this happening to them. Write down all the responses on the flip chart.

2. Ask the participants to brainstorm other ways of acknowledging a customer's feelings. Explain brainstorming rules: Keep the flow going. Do not discuss ideas until they are all on the flip chart. No idea is too silly. Do not give feedback on ideas. Do not criticize ideas.

3. Find a partner to role play. Explain the rules like this: "One of you will play the role of customer and the other the role of service provider. The customer has brought a product back for the second time. (The customer can choose the product.). The first time, it was repaired; now the customer wants to exchange it. It is the role of the service provider to acknowledge the customer's feelings. Explain that the participants can use the ideas created from the brainstorming session and that are now displayed on the flip chart. After 5 minutes, ask the pair to switch roles. The person now playing the customer chooses a different product.

4. Ask for feedback. How did it feel? What were the problems? What worked?

5. Hand out Exercise 28.2. Ask participants to complete it and give feedback.

6. Provide a summary. Answer any questions before wrapping up.

# Acknowledge Customer's Feelings

*"I understand how you must feel, and I apologize.
Please tell me what would make it better for you."*

# EXERCISE 28.2: SUPER SERVICE ACTION PLAN

The actions I will take as a result of this activity are:

1. _____
   _____
   _____
   _____

2. _____
   _____
   _____
   _____

3. _____
   _____
   _____

4. _____
   _____
   _____

5. _____
   _____
   _____

6. _____
   _____
   _____

I will review this action plan on: _____     _____
                                                  (date)                                        (signed)

## Activity 29
# When to Call In the Manager

It doesn't matter whether customers are right or wrong.
They need to air their complaints.

## Background and Purpose

There are always times when a manager needs to be called in to help with a situation. Knowing when to call and when not to call is key to saving time, helping the customer, and letting the service provider know what is expected of them.

This activity will identify crucial times when to call in a manager. And crucial times when not to call in a manager.

## Objectives

By the end of this activity, participants will be able to:

1. Identify when to call in a manager.

2. Identify when not to call in a manager.

## Time

Approximately 1 hour

## Materials Required

1. Overheads 29.1 and 29.2

2. Exercise 29.3

## Mini Lecture

There are times when you have to call in the manager. A manager can help bring a new perspective to the situation. A manager can also give the customer more confidence that the problem will be solved.

It is very appropriate to call the manager if the customer is angry, and you have tried every solution possible, and the customer is still not satisfied.

However, calling in the manager may be admitting defeat too soon. Perhaps you haven't made the customer feel that you really care or have the authority to solve the problem. In other words, you don't trust you, and the customer doesn't trust you!

## Steps to Follow

1. Show Overhead 29.1. Explain that there are some situations when a manager should be called in.

2. Show Overhead 29.2. Explain that calling in a manager should be a last resort.

3. Ask the group to brainstorm the problems that they encounter with customers. Use brainstorming rules: No idea is too silly. No discussing ideas until the end. No criticizing ideas. Allow for a free flow of ideas to develop. Write down all the ideas on a flip chart.

4. Ask the participants to work in teams of 3 to 4. Ask them to choose two ideas from the brainstorming session. Have the first idea develop into a situation in which the manager needs to be called in. The second idea develops into a situation in which the manager does not need to be called in. Tell the teams they have 20 minutes to come up with the two scenarios. They then will have 5 to 10 minutes each (depending on time and the size of the group) to present their ideas and solutions to the group.

5. Ask for feedback at the end of each presentation.

6. Hand out Exercise 29.3. Ask the participants to complete the exercise. (If you have time, you can ask for feedback and comments about the last exercise.)

7. When every group has made its presentation, provide a summary and wrap up.

# When to Call In the Manager

■ When you have no authority to provide the solution.

■ When you have explored every solution and nothing is satisfactory to the customer.

# Why Calling a Manager Is a Last Resort

- If you *think* you lack the power
  to resolve the problem,
  you *do* lack the power.

- You are showing the customer
  that you cannot
  resolve problems.

# EXERCISE 29.3: SUPER SERVICE ACTION PLAN

The actions I will take as a result of this activity are:

1. _____
   _____
   _____
   _____

2. _____
   _____
   _____
   _____

3. _____
   _____
   _____
   _____

4. _____
   _____
   _____
   _____

5. _____
   _____
   _____

6. _____
   _____
   _____

I will review this action plan on: _____    _____
                                      (date)                                         (signed)

## Activity 30
# Reach Agreement

Incorporate the customer's ideas into your solution.

## Background and Purpose

Every company wants to have an agreeable relationship with its customers. This activity is aimed toward helping customer service providers understand why. Why is it so important for a customer to reach agreement with a company? Why is it so important to have employees reach agreements between themselves? This activity answers those questions.

## Objectives

By the end of this activity, participants will be able to:

1. Understand the importance of reaching agreement.

2. Understand the law of cause and effect.

## Time

Approximately 45 minutes

## Materials Required

1. Overheads 30.1 and 30.3

2. Exercises 30.2 and 30.4

## Mini Lecture

In order to reach agreement, we must be of one mind. We achieve this by listening and by understanding the law of cause and effect. Wanting to reach agreement means that we want agreement more than we want conflict. We want harmony more than we want arguments. Sometimes it is difficult to understand this concept when we are so caught up in winning. The idea behind reaching agreement is that both parties can win.

We are not saying that we lie down and agree about everything the customer wants. There is always something that the customer has to give in return. It could be money, it could be training support, and it could be future orders. Reaching agreement means both sides get what they need.

## Steps to Follow

1. Show Overhead 30.1. Explain that reaching agreement often depends on the situation.

2. Ask the participants to group into teams of 4. Give each team copies of Exercise 30.2 (one per individual for taking notes). Ask them to come up with the answers and be prepared to present their ideas after 20 minutes.

3. Show Overhead 30.3. Explain that the law of cause and effect is a physical law that works on another level also. Everything we think, other people read. So when we say one thing and think another, most people know it! Reaching agreement is really about reaching agreement with yourself. Do you agree to work for this company? Do you agree to do the best job? Do you agree to be helpful to customers? Do you agree to reach agreement more often than not?

   Ask for feedback and lead a group discussion about the importance of reaching agreement. If people have questions about the benefits of disagreement, ask them how it feels to be disagreeable. How does it feel to be in the company of people who disagree all the time?

4. Hand out Exercise 30.4. Ask participants to complete it, and then ask if anyone would like to share answers.

5. Provide a summary and answer any questions before wrapping up.

# How You Reach Agreement Depends On:

- Company policy

- Whether the customer needs training on product use

- Whether the customer has abused the product or service in the past, or is doing so now

- The costs involved (actual cost versus goodwill)

# EXERCISE 30.2: TEAM ACTIVITY

Discuss the following questions within your team, and then answer them. Be prepared to present your answers to the group.

1. How much does your product or service cost to repair?

2. How much does your product or service cost to replace?

3. How important are customers to your company?

4. Do certain customers deserve special treatment? (Please identify situations or customers to back up your answer.)

5. How loyal are your customers and how does this affect your ability to reach agreement?

# Law of Cause and Effect

For every action there is an equal
and opposite reaction.

Every time we feel disagreement,
we send disagreement out
and we get disagreement back.

Every time we feel agreement,
we send agreement out
and we get agreement back.

# EXERCISE 30.4: SUPER SERVICE ACTION PLAN

The actions I will take as a result of this activity are:

1. _____

   _____

   _____

   _____


2. _____

   _____

   _____

   _____


3. _____

   _____

   _____

   _____


4. _____

   _____

   _____

   _____


5. _____

   _____

   _____


6. _____

   _____

   _____


I will review this action plan on: _____     _____
                                        (date)                        (signed)

# Activity 31
# Win–Win Solutions

Taking action not only helps you and the person you are helping; it leads you to enlightenment.

## Background and Purpose

There are many books about negotiating and how to use tactics to negotiate what you want. This activity is about seeking to win from both sides of the table. If we are straightforward and honest with ourselves we can create a workforce that promotes openness, kindness, and wise communication.

## Objectives

By the end of this activity, participants will be able to:

1.  Understand what a win–win situation looks like and how it will benefit them.

2.  Understand the difference between empathy and sympathy.

3.  Know how to seek win–win solutions.

## Time

Approximately 90 minutes

## Materials Required

1.  Overheads 31.1 and 31.2

2.  Role Play Scenarios 31.3 A and 31.3 B

3.  Exercise 31.4

## Mini Lecture

It's hard to seek a win–win solution when your mind is full of tactics and countertactics. It is much easier when you come from a place of truth and listen to what the customer needs and wants. This is not to say that we give everything away. In a world where some customers sue for slipping on a wet floor (and sometimes they are the ones who spilled the water deliberately), honesty is still the best policy because lies become too complicated to hold onto, and almost always get found out.

Imagine that your customers were close friends or relatives. You would probably want them to be happy, satisfied, and content. You would really listen to their issues and want to help resolve them. If your friends had a grievance, you would actually understand why they were hurting. You would show compassion and empathy for them because they were close to you. It's hard to have this respect for a stranger, but it's what we need to do. However, we need to do it in such a way that we detach ourselves from the personality of the customer.

If the customer is angry, we cannot take on the anger. If the customer is happy, we cannot assume that he or she will always be happy. We must be detached from the emotions of the customer. We do this by listening, empathizing, finding a solution that works for both us and the customer, and then moving on to the next customer.

## Steps to Follow

1. Show Overhead 31.1. Explain that acknowledging customers' feelings does not mean that we have to "take on" their problems. We can empathize and still be detached from their problems. If we take the problem on board, we lose our perspective and are unable to help. If we keep calm and detached, we can remain far enough away from the problem to look for and find a solution.

2. Show Overhead 31.2. Explain that there is often interference in communication. Just like a radio that isn't tuned in properly, if we are not tuned into the customers, we don't really hear what they are saying. Ask the class for some examples of each of the barriers: physical barriers (noise, lack of time); emotional barriers (personal problems, stress of work); knowledge barriers (don't know about the product or service); language barriers (jargon, speaks a different language, or uses a different vocabulary).

   Ask the class for solutions to these barriers: Listen, repeat what they have said for your understanding, use their words, and use empathy.

3. Distribute Role Play Scenario 31.3 A. Ask the participants to pair up and role play the scenario described. Allow 5 minutes for this exercise. When they have finished, distribute Role Play Scenario 31.3 B. Ask participants to exchange roles and play the new scenario. When the role plays are finished, ask for feedback and lead a discussion with the entire group.

   Ask the following questions:

   a.  How did you create a win–win situation?

   b.  What worked best?

   c.  What did not work?

   d.  Which role did you prefer playing and why?

   e.  How will this exercise help you in the future?

4. Hand out Exercise 31.4. Ask participants to complete the exercise and then ask if anyone will share observations with the rest of the class.

5. Provide a brief summary and answer any questions before wrapping up.

# Empathy is not the same as sympathy.

**Sympathy means you take on the problem.**

**Empathy means you acknowledge the problem, but you do not take ownership!**

# Communication

## Interference occurs through different barriers:

- Physical Barriers

- Emotional Barriers

- Knowledge Barriers

- Language Barriers

# ROLE PLAY SCENARIO 31.3 A: SEEKING WIN–WIN SOLUTIONS

Please read the following scenario. One person will role play the part of the customer, and the other person will role play the part of the customer service provider.

## CUSTOMER

You are a customer returning a product that is defective. You bought it on sale, and there was a large notice saying, "No return on sale items." However, you are a loyal and regular customer, and you do not normally return items. This is a big-ticket item for you (you can determine the item yourself), and you feel that you should have either a full refund or an exchange for the same or a similar product.

## CUSTOMER SERVICE PROVIDER

You are the customer service provider. Your job is to seek a win–win solution.

# ROLE PLAY SCENARIO 31.3 B: SEEKING WIN–WIN SOLUTIONS

Please read the following scenario. One person will role play the part of the customer, and the other person will role play the part of the customer service provider.

## CUSTOMER

You are a customer at a restaurant. You are a regular here and have booked a table for six. It is your partner's special birthday. The receptionist informs you that the reservation was not written down. The restaurant is now full, and you will have to wait 40 minutes for a table. Not only that...you wanted the round table, and that is unavailable for the entire evening.

## CUSTOMER SERVICE PROVIDER

You are the customer service provider. Your job is to seek a win–win solution.

# EXERCISE 31.4: SUPER SERVICE ACTION PLAN

The actions I will take as a result of this activity are:

1. _____

   _____

   _____

   _____

2. _____

   _____

   _____

   _____

3. _____

   _____

   _____

   _____

4. _____

   _____

   _____

   _____

5. _____

   _____

   _____

   _____

6. _____

   _____

   _____

I will review this action plan on: _____     _____

                                 (date)                                   (signed)

Sometimes a conversation can flow smoothly, sometimes not. Miscommunication is a big problem within a company, because it stops the workflow. It is nonproductive and creates bad feelings.

When miscommunication occurs with a customer, there is the potential to lose business. This activity shows that one of the best solutions is to listen and build on the other person's proposal.

## Objectives

By the end of this activity, participants will be able to:

1. Understand the concept of mirroring.

2. Know how to use mirroring effectively.

3. Create tools for enabling conversations to flow smoothly.

## Time

Approximately 2 hours

## Materials Required

1. Overhead 32.1

2. Exercise 32.2

## Mini Lecture

Have you ever been in conversation with someone when the conversation seemed to flow beautifully and you didn't know why? It's often because that person was mirroring something that you like in yourself. It is the same when we listen to a speaker. If he or she is saying something that we agree with, we nod our heads in agreement, as if we were the ones who came up with the idea first.

Usually the reason we dislike people is because they mirror the things we don't like in ourselves. "There's something I don't like about that person,"

## Activity 32

# Build on the Customer's Proposal

Added value means going the extra mile or going beyond the call of duty.

usually translates into, "That person is showing a side of me that I dislike and I don't even want to acknowledge it!"

You may have heard that we shed our bodies every seven years. It's true! Every seven years, you are in a completely new body: new cells, new everything. Perhaps the only reason we get old is that we hang on so very dearly to our old ways of being.

Sit and think about shedding your old self. Become the person you want to become now! There's no better time to do it. When you have an open heart you can help your customers from a place that truly wants to help, rather than from a place that really wants to help only yourself.

When the customer proposes something, it's not a good idea to say, "No, we have to do it this way." Instead, build on the proposal. It takes some thought to do that, but once you get into the habit, your conversations and communication with people will flow much easier, and your life will flow better as a result.

## Steps to Follow

1. Show Overhead 32.1. Explain that these solutions are not written in any particular order. You could start by incorporating the customer's ideas into your solutions.

2. Team Activity: Ask the group to form teams of 4. Allow 4 to 5 minutes for them to think of a common customer problem. (This can be an internal or external customer problem. However, no individual names should be used.)

   Allow a further 5 to 10 minutes for them to create solutions to their problems.

   Give the teams 15 minutes to write the following:

   a.  An explanation of why they offered this solution.

   b.  Questions to gain a better understanding of the problem.

   c.  Some ideas or solutions the customer may have that can be incorporated into the team solution.

   Ask each team to present its problem, solution, and answers to a, b, and c. Allow 5 to 10 minutes to work on the presentations, and 5 to 10 minutes to present to the rest of the group.

   Between presentations, ask for and provide feedback.

3. Distribute Exercise 32.2. Ask the participants to complete the exercise. Ask for volunteers who are willing to share their thoughts.

4. Provide a brief summary and answer any questions before wrapping up.

## Discussion Points

1. What does it feel like to think that the people you do not like may be mirroring something you do not like in yourself?

2. What are some ways to overcome this mirroring? (Possible answers include: Stop being so defensive. Come from your heart instead of your head. See their positive qualities.)

# Build on the Customer's Proposal

- Explain to the customer why you offered the solution and how it will help the situation.

- Ask questions to gain a better understanding of the situation.

- Check your understanding by explaining the problem in your own words.

- Incorporate the customer's ideas into your solution.

- Build and communicate on the joint ideas.

# EXERCISE 32.2: SUPER SERVICE ACTION PLAN

The actions I will take as a result of this activity are:

1. _____

_____

_____

_____

2. _____

_____

_____

_____

3. _____

_____

_____

_____

4. _____

_____

_____

5. _____

_____

_____

6. _____

_____

_____

I will review this action plan on: _____    _____
                                        (date)                              (signed)

## Activity 33
# Being Creative

## Background and Purpose

Companies that foster creativity in their employees are not only opening the doorway to new and better ideas; the employees feel better about themselves and their environment. When a company stifles creativity, it is putting the lid on endless opportunities for new growth.

This activity encourages letting that creativity out. It shows people how to be creative and how to enjoy success.

## Objectives

By the end of this activity, participants will be able to:

1. Let go of thoughts that they are not creative.

2. Tap into new creative areas.

3. Understand that everyone has the potential to be creative.

## Time

Approximately 20 minutes

## Materials Required

1. Overheads 33.1 and 33.2

2. A soft (e.g., Nerf™) ball

3. Exercise 33.3

## Mini Lecture

We all have huge amounts of creativity; some people are simply more open to using it than others. Creativity is being open to new ideas. Sometimes, we think that creativity in business is different from creativity in the artist's studio; not so. Creativity is creativity, wherever it occurs.

If you get into a slump, that becomes visible to everyone around you; be creative in finding your way out.

To serve others is ultimately to serve ourselves, because when we open our hearts, our spirit grows and becomes stronger.

## Steps to Follow

1. Show Overhead 33.1. Explain that we sometimes ignore what worked when we were very young. We may have been great artists, and drawing could be a way to tap into our creative flow. Acknowledge what is not working now. Is there something in the way of your being creative? What is it? Can it be addressed? What can you do differently to expand your mind? What resources do you have? Be creative in thinking of resources.

   Ask the group for feedback on these suggestions. Ask for a volunteer to talk about what (creatively) has worked in the past and what is not working now. See if you can find a link between the two. For example, someone who wrote very well early in life may need an outlet for writing now. That person should look for areas in the job or company where he or she can use those writing skills.

2. Show Overhead 33.2. Explain that these are suggestions. Ask the group for other ways to have fun getting out of a rut.

3. Ask the group to form a circle. As you throw the soft ball around the circle, ask the person who catches the ball to come up with something he or she will do differently to get out of a rut. (You can do this a few times with each person, so they all come up with more than one creative activity.)

   When everyone has had a chance to catch the ball and answer the question, ask for feedback. Example: How did you feel when you had to come up with a fast answer? What are the lessons to be learned here? How can we help each other be more creative?

4. Distribute Exercise 33.3 and ask participants to complete it. Ask for volunteers to share their thoughts.

5. Provide a brief summary and answer any questions before wrapping up.

## Discussion Points

1. How can being creative help in your job?

2. What have you noticed other people doing to be creative?

3. Is there something that you have always wanted to do creatively for your job but haven't gotten around to doing?

# How to Find Your Way to Creativity

- What worked in the past?

- What is not working now?

- What can I do differently?

- What resources do I have?

# Have Fun Getting Out of Your Rut

- Dress differently for a day.

- Style your hair differently and see how it makes you feel.

- Find a good joke to tell everyone.

- Eat different foods outside of your normal choice.

- Skip the coffee and find a new way to wake up.

- If you brush your teeth starting on the top left— try brushing from the bottom right.

# EXERCISE 33.3: SUPER SERVICE ACTION PLAN

The actions I will take as a result of this activity are:

1. _____

   _____

   _____

   _____

2. _____

   _____

   _____

   _____

3. _____

   _____

   _____

4. _____

   _____

   _____

5. _____

   _____

   _____

6. _____

   _____

   _____

I will review this action plan on: _____    _____
                                          (date)                                (signed)

## Activity 34
# Tactfully Redirect

## Background and Purpose

Being tactful is one key to a person's success in customer service. This activity allows all participants to understand their level of tact in a nonconfrontational way.

## Objectives

By the end of this activity, participants will be able to:

1. Understand how others perceive them as tactful or nontactful people.

2. Understand the importance of using tact.

## Time

Approximately 1 hour

## Materials Required

1. Overhead 34.1

2. One piece of Play-Doh for each participant

3. Exercise 34.2

## Mini Lecture

It's not always easy serving our internal customers, especially if we know them very well. It is easy to get complacent. Sometimes we are too busy and want people to just get on with it.

Sometimes we need to talk things out or hear another opinion. Sometimes we are so involved with the issue, we can't see it clearly any more. This is when we need to tactfully redirect the customer.

## Steps to Follow

1. Show Overhead 34.1. Explain that tactfully redirecting does not mean saying "No." It means saying, "Yes, and have you considered this possibility?"

2. Hand out the Play-Doh and give each participant 5 minutes to build a structure of what tact looks like to them.

   Ask them to form groups of 5 to 6. Each person will have 2 minutes to explain his or her "tact" structure. They should explain why they like it and what it means to them. It is the group's task to provide tactful feedback about how the structure could be reshaped. Each person must provide feedback tactfully.

   When each person has had a turn to present a structure and has received feedback from the group, ask the group the following questions:

   a. How did it feel?

   b. What worked and what did not work about tactfully redirecting?

   c. How can we improve our tactful communication skills?

   d. When is tact important?

   e. How will this exercise change your communication skills?

3. Hand out Exercise 34.2 and ask participants to complete it.

4. Provide a brief summary and answer any questions before wrapping up the session.

# How to Tactfully Redirect

- Look at all the possible solutions.

- Decide on one solution that works best for both parties.

- Build enthusiasm about the one solution that works for both parties.

# EXERCISE 34.2: SUPER SERVICE ACTION PLAN

The actions I will take as a result of this activity are:

1. _____

_____

_____

_____

2. _____

_____

_____

_____

3. _____

_____

_____

4. _____

_____

_____

5. _____

_____

_____

6. _____

_____

_____

I will review this action plan on: _____      _____
                                                              (date)                                                    (signed)

## Activity 35

# How Not to Give Away the Shop

One of the key components of selling is having great energy.

## Background and Purpose

It's great to give customers what they want, but if they want too much, the company will end up losing profits. This activity teaches the importance of giving great service and keeping the company profitable.

## Objectives

By the end of this activity, participants will be able to:

- Understand the value of the company's product or service and what employees can and cannot provide.

## Time

Approximately 3 hours

## Materials Required

1. Overheads 35.1, 35.2, and 35.3
2. Exercises 35.4, 35.5, and 35.6

## Mini Lecture

How not to give away the shop comes down to making wise decisions. It's about making a great proposal that keeps both parties in business. Sometimes the customer can be overly demanding, but because we want to provide Super Service, we should never tell customers they are being unreasonable—or should we?

If you bottle up resentment and anger, you will feel ill. Frustration and anger are emotions that flare up when we feel challenged. We become like knights of old: our shields come up and our words act like spears (thrown at the other person from behind the shield). We would be better to keep our shields down, detach from our emotions, and look at the situation objectively. Emotional reactions not only hurt us, they hurt the people around us. So the answer is to detach from your emotions. Breathe in, and take another deep breath before you react.

## Steps to Follow

1.  Show Overhead 35.1. Explain that the purpose of this question is to have you look at anger. Dealing with anger or resentment means releasing it as you experience it, moment by moment. This does not mean spilling your emotions all over your customers, internal or external. It means detaching from your emotions and taking a breath while you look at the situation from a cooler vantage point.

2.  Show Overhead 35.2. Explain that the customers' proposal or solution may not truly answer their needs. You must ask yourself, "Will it satisfy and resolve the issue for them?" and, "How will it affect me or my company?"

3.  Show Overhead 35.3. Explain that we can use phrases that show the customer our "good heart and intentions." We are talking about open-hearted wisdom. Here is the clue: Every action is preceded by a thought, so we have to think good thoughts before we speak.

4.  Distribute Exercise 35.4. Ask each participant to complete it, while you continue showing Overhead 35.3.

5.  Ask the group to form teams of 4 to 5 and distribute Exercise 35.5. Allow 10 minutes for them to read it and answer the questions as a team.

    Feedback questions:

    a.  What did you learn from this exercise?

    b.  How does it apply to your job?

    c.  Can you see how being calm can help a situation?

6.  Using a flip chart, ask the group to brainstorm situations in which the customer expects more than you could provide. Allow 10 minutes of brainstorming while you write down the answers.

    Ask them to go into different groups of 4 to 5 people. Allow 20 minutes for each group to choose two of the brainstorming situations and create two scenarios in which the customer service provider gives customer satisfaction without giving the shop away.

    Ask each team to role play each scenario. Two people role play one of the situations, and the other two role play the other situation. Allow 2 minutes per scenario.

    Provide feedback as appropriate.

7.  Hand out Exercise 35.6 and ask participants to complete it. Ask if any volunteers would like to share their thoughts.

8.  Provide a brief summary and answer any questions before wrapping up.

# Imagine

## a bottle labeled

## "Anger."

## Would you swallow it?

# You do not have to do
# whatever
# the customer suggests.
# However,
# you do have to
# be on the customer's side.

# Good Thoughts

**Think:** We are on the same side of the fence.

**Say:** "I like your idea about…"

**Think:** We want the same thing.

**Say:** "We can work on your suggestion to…"

**Think:** I want the best for both.

**Say:** "From my experience, I think your best option is…"

**Think:** One small step is all it takes.

**Say:** "I like your idea, and perhaps we can also…"

**EXERCISE 35.4**

Choose one of the example phrases from the Good Thoughts overhead. Copy your example below in very large writing. When you get back to work, pin the thought where you can see it. Refer to it throughout the day as a reminder that everything begins with a thought. Good thoughts are as easy to have as bad thoughts. It just takes conscious choice.

## EXERCISE 35.5

Please read the following story and answer the questions that follow it as a group.

Here is a story of a flight attendant. A passenger in first class ordered a special low-carbohydrate meal. The order had not been processed and his food had not arrived on board the plane. He was so angry that he threatened to throw his meal (the standard one that everyone else was eating) at the steward who was serving him. The situation was so bad that the captain had been informed and the police had been alerted to meet the flight when it landed.

Another flight attendant who had been standing by decided to act. She went up to the passenger and stood quietly and calmly beside him. "I can see that you are really angry," she said.

The passenger looked at her and said, "Yes, I'm angry!"

The flight attendant continued to stand beside him and talk to him calmly and listened to what he had to say. Eventually, the man took his seat again. When they landed, the police allowed him to leave the aircraft without further incident. Before he left, he went to the flight attendant who had assisted him and said, "Thank you for listening to me. No one listens to me anymore!"

1. What was the main reason that the passenger calmed down?

2. Have you ever been in a similar situation, heard about a situation, or witnessed a situation involving a customer who was angry?

3. How was it resolved?

# EXERCISE 35.6: SUPER SERVICE ACTION PLAN

The actions I will take as a result of this activity are:

1. _____
   _____
   _____
   _____

2. _____
   _____
   _____
   _____

3. _____
   _____
   _____

4. _____
   _____
   _____

5. _____
   _____
   _____

6. _____
   _____
   _____

I will review this action plan on: _____     _____
                                        (date)                              (signed)

## Background and Purpose

Customers need to be understood, and more importantly, they need to know that they are understood. Checking understanding with customers gives them an opportunity to confirm that your solution meets their needs. It takes more than just restating the problem. It means checking that you understand the problem and have found the right solution.

This activity outlines six easy steps for checking understanding.

## Objectives

By the end of this activity, participants will be able to:

■ Name and use the six steps for checking understanding.

## Time

Approximately 2 hours

## Materials Required

1. Overheads 36.1 and 36.2

2. Role Play Scenarios 36.3 A and 36.3 B

3. Handout 36.4

4. Exercise 36.5

5. One softball

## Mini Lecture

We all need to feel understood. Customers are no different. If we feel understood, we will continue the conversation. If we do not feel understood, we may not stop talking, but we will probably stop talking to that particular person!

Basically, we all want the same things: security, to feel liked or loved, and to experience human kindness. We want to be treated well, to feel important, to

# Activity 36
# Check Understanding

When you explain to customers *how* their service needs will be met by your organization, they feel in control.

feel that we made a good deal and that we were not taken advantage of. If we pay money for something, we want it to work; and if it does not work, we want it to be replaced.

## Steps to Follow

1.  Show Overhead 36.1. Explain the six steps to checking understanding:

    1.  **Make sure the customer understands your intentions.** The customer should know what your specific job is and what you can do to help. There is nothing worse for a customer than to explain to the wrong person what he or she wants. Let the customer know what you can do to help. If the customer needs to speak with someone else, you can redirect the call.

    2.  **Be prepared for customer input.** The customer wants to make sure you understand his or her needs, so be prepared to listen.

    3.  **Verify the facts.** Rephrase what has been said. "If I understand you correctly, you would like the top window replaced, but you are satisfied with everything else."

    4.  **Check for agreement to the plan.** It's no good if you are happy with the plan and your customer is not! Before going ahead with any solution, check for agreement that you are headed in the right direction.

    5.  **Accept responsibility.** If you are at fault, accept responsibility. Putting up a great defense will only make the customer want to knock it down.

    6.  **End on a positive note.** This can be a simple, "Thank you for letting us know about this problem. We want to get it right for our customers."

2.  Show Overhead 36.2 and explain that we cannot understand people, and specifically our customers, unless we understand ourselves. What makes us tick? What motivates us? What makes us get up in the morning? Once we understand these things, then we can apply that knowledge to our customers.

3.  Ask the group to form a circle. Throw the softball to someone and as you throw it, ask them, "What motivates your customer?" That person in turn throws the ball to someone else and asks the same question. Each person must come up with a different answer, and every person in the circle must have at least one turn.

4.  When you have finished, go to the flip chart and ask the group to repeat the answers as you record them. When you have recorded most of the answers, ask the group, "Are these the same things that motivate you?" Explain that we are all the same. Most of us want to feel accepted and we want to feel secure. Our customers want the same things, so we have to make them feel accepted and secure.

5.  Ask participants to form groups of 4. Give them 10 minutes to come up with at least five ways to make their customers feel accepted and secure. Ask each group to share ideas with the whole group.

6.  Ask participants to find a partner. Give each pair one copy of Role Play Scenario 36.3 A and 36.3 B. One should play the role of the customer, and one

of the customer service provider. Give the pairs 5 minutes to role play the first scenario. After 5 minutes, they should swap roles and role play the second scenario.

7. When they have all completed their role plays, ask the group for feedback. How did they feel in the different roles? What worked? What did not work? What can they do differently?

8. Provide each person with a copy of Handout 36.4. Explain that they can pin this checklist up to remind them of the steps involved in checking understanding.

9. Hand out Exercise 36.5 and ask participants to complete it. If you have time, ask if anyone is willing to share thoughts.

10. Provide a brief summary and answer any last questions before wrapping up.

# Check Understanding

1. Make sure the customer understands your intentions.

2. Be prepared for customer input.

3. Verify the facts.

4. Check for agreement of plan.

5. Accept responsibility.

6. End on a positive note.

# What Motivates Us?

1. What makes us tick?

2. What makes us get up in the morning?

3. What is the difference between ourselves and our customers?

# ROLE PLAY SCENARIO 36.3 A: CHECK UNDERSTANDING

There are two scenarios. Both are written here for you; your partner has a copy of the scenarios. In the first one, you will play the role of customer. In the second one, you will play the role of customer service provider.

## Scenario 1
## CUSTOMER

You bought an entire computer system including a printer and scanner from a large discount warehouse computer store five weeks ago. The salesperson told you it would include an internal Zip drive. You got it home, set it up, threw out the boxes, and went on an extended business trip. It wasn't until you returned that you realized the Zip drive was missing.

You have no proof that the system was supposed to have a Zip drive, but you know the salesperson's name was Tom Blake.

You have come to the store to find out if you can, a) exchange the system for one with a Zip drive; b) get a free Zip drive for the inconvenience; or c) be credited with the price of a Zip drive the next time you buy software.

## Scenario 2
## CUSTOMER SERVICE PROVIDER

You are a flight attendant working for a major airline. You are standing at the gate and have just announced that boarding can commence. You have asked first class passengers and executive premier passengers to board first. This is a full flight and you have let through ten first class passengers already. Now a person with one executive premier card is expecting to board along with a spouse and two young children.

The early boarding rule is that premier executives are only allowed to take one passenger with them.

You tell the person to take the two children through, but the spouse will have to wait with the other passengers until that row is called. You are only following the rules!

# ROLE PLAY SCENARIO 36.3 B: CHECK UNDERSTANDING

There are two scenarios. Both are written here for you; your partner has a copy of the scenarios. In the first one, you will play the role of customer service provider. In the second one, you will play the role of customer.

## Scenario 1
### CUSTOMER SERVICE PROVIDER

You are a new employee for a discount warehouse computer store. You can only exchange computer systems if the company is at fault.

The customer in front of you bought an entire computer system including a printer and scanner from the store five weeks ago. The customer says it was supposed to have an internal Zip drive installed. The salesperson, Tom Blake, has since left the company, and the customer has no proof that the system was supposed to have a Zip drive.

You want to do a good job for the company and the customer; What do you do?

## Scenario 2
### CUSTOMER

You are standing at the gate of a major airline. The flight attendant has just announced that boarding can commence. They have asked first class passengers and executive premier passengers to board first. You have an executive premier card. You are with your spouse and two young children.

You and your family have been traveling since 4 a.m. You are all very tired, especially the children. Since this is a full flight, you are very glad to be able to board first and get your family settled. You would be very unhappy if you were told that your spouse could not board early with you—you need help with the children!

# HANDOUT 36.4: CHECKLIST FOR CHECKING UNDERSTANDING

Pin this checklist where you can see it to remind you of the steps involved in checking understanding.

1. Make sure the customer understands what you intend to do: "So to clarify, tomorrow at 9 a.m., the service engineer will come and look at the system; is this correct?"

2. Be prepared for customer input.

3. This is your last chance to verify facts, so check your notes.

4. Check for agreement to the plan: "Will these steps meet your needs?"

5. Accept responsibility: "Call me if there are any further issues."

6. End on a positive note: "I'm glad it worked out."

# EXERCISE 36.5: SUPER SERVICE ACTION PLAN

The actions I will take as a result of this activity are:

1. _____

   _____

   _____

   _____

2. _____

   _____

   _____

   _____

3. _____

   _____

   _____

   _____

4. _____

   _____

   _____

   _____

5. _____

   _____

   _____

   _____

6. _____

   _____

   _____

   _____

I will review this action plan on: _____     _____
                                          (date)                        (signed)

## Background and Purpose

The military uses Standard Operating Procedures as a way of ensuring that certain tasks are carried out in a certain way. It helps people to perform without too much thought. While this can be very useful in times of battle, it is not always useful when dealing with people one on one.

This activity allows the participants to recognize how they are interacting with their customers. It shows them when they are thinking and when they are not thinking. At the end of the activity, they will no longer act without thinking; instead they will think before acting.

## Activity 37

# Standard Operating Procedure

## Objectives

By the end of this activity, participants will be able to:

1. Think before acting.

2. Become aware of the habits they want to change.

3. Look for more than they think is there.

## Time

Approximately 45 minutes

## Materials Required

1. Overheads 37.1 and 37.2

2. One penny (preferably a new one) for each of the participants

3. Exercise 37.3

## Mini Lecture

We may not think it, but we all have standard operating procedures: habits we have become so used to that we no longer think about them. These habits dictate whether we stand and argue, or simply walk away. The problem with these kind of habits is, that we no longer "see" what is really there. We think we know everything, so we stop looking. When we see our customers, we think we know them by the way they speak, or walk, or talk.

## Steps to Follow

1. Show Overhead 37.1. Explain that people go through four basic stages of learning when they want to overcome or change a habit:

   a. First we become aware that we need or want to learn something different. If our standard operating procedure is to be judgmental with our customers, the first step is to know and recognize that we are being judgmental.

   b. The second step is awkwardness. When you become aware of being judgmental (or whatever the habit is) and you decide not to be, you will have to stop and think before speaking or reacting spontaneously, out of habit.

   c. The third step is skill. It takes skill to go through feeling awkward and knowing that you really want to change your habit. It means that you have to be more awake—to be in the present moment without thinking about being somewhere else.

   d. The fourth step is habit. When you change one habit, you eventually develop a different habit, hopefully a better one that will serve both you and your customers better.

2. Hand each participant a penny. Allow each individual 5 minutes to make a list of all the distinguishable characteristics of the common penny.

3. Show Overhead 37.2. Ask for a show of hands to find out how many individuals scored correctly. Ask these questions:

   a. How can individuals see something as common as a penny almost daily, yet not "see" its characteristics?

   b. How can we increase our individual (and daily) attention?

   c. What does this tell you about our way of thinking that we already know all there is to know about everything, even our customers?

4. Ask participants to complete Exercise 37.3 and ask if anyone is willing to share ideas.

5. Provide a brief summary and answer any questions before wrapping up.

# To Change a Habit

1. Be aware of the habit.
2. Be willing to be awkward.
3. Learn the skill of changing.
4. Form a different habit.

# What's on a Penny?

## Front Side

1. "In God We Trust"
2. "Liberty"
3. Date
4. Mint mark (under date, sometimes)
5. President Lincoln's portrait facing to his left

## Back Side

6. "United States of America"
7. "One Cent"
8. "E Pluribus Unum"
9. Lincoln Memorial (12 columns)
10. Lincoln statue in middle of columns

## General

11. It is copper colored.
12. The rim around the edge on both sides is raised.
13. The front and back are inverted with respect to each other.
14. The diameter is 3/4 inch.
15. The thickness is approximately 1/16 inch.
16. Its weight is approximately 1/6 ounce.
17. The external rim is smooth on the outside.

# EXERCISE 37.3: SUPER SERVICE ACTION PLAN

The actions I will take as a result of this activity are:

1. _____
   _____
   _____
   _____

2. _____
   _____
   _____
   _____

3. _____
   _____
   _____

4. _____
   _____
   _____

5. _____
   _____
   _____

6. _____
   _____
   _____

I will review this action plan on: _____    _____
                                         (date)                    (signed)

# Activity 38
# Manage Expectations

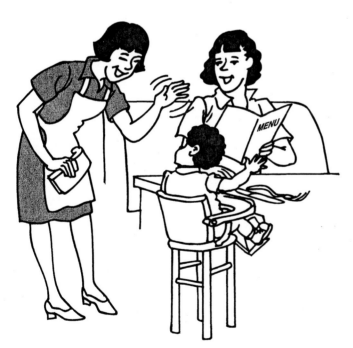

Connecting with a customer's heart and soul means appreciating your customers as fully rounded human beings with all the joy, family issues, money scares, and work problems that every one of us experiences from time to time.

## Background and Purpose

We all expect certain things to happen; and customers are no different. It is when things happen differently from the way we expected that we get into trouble. The purpose of this activity is to enable people to manage the expectations of their customers right at the beginning of the communication.

This exercise must be done in an atmosphere of trust and openness.

## Objectives

By the end of this activity, participants will be able to:

1. Understand what the customer expects.

2. Manage those expectations.

## Time

Approximately 45 minutes

## Materials Required

1. Flip chart and markers

2. Exercise 38.1

## Mini Lecture

When we know what is going to happen, we feel in control. When we don't know what is going to happen, we feel out of control and very uncomfortable. This can lead to frustration and anger.

If you need to hand over a customer's problem to the billing department, be sure to tell the customer and the billing department. Make it easy for your customer, and your life will become easier. If customers feel you think they are not important, they will start to make themselves important—and that often means getting mad.

## Steps to Follow

1. Ask the participants to form teams of 5. Give them 10 minutes to make a "wish list" of all the things they would change about customers' expectations. For example, "I wish customers knew which department to ask for" or, "I wish customers didn't expect free service after the warranty is over."

   Now ask each group to choose the three most important wishes. (Write all of them down on the flip chart.) Next, conduct a brainstorming session to provide solutions to the most urgent wishes. For example, if the wish is that customer's know which department to ask for (this is a recurring and difficult problem), the solution could be customer education, perhaps printing a list for customers of who and where to call. If customers always expect free service when the warranty is over, the solution could be to sell the customers an extended warranty at the point of sale.

   Key point: The solutions should be things that make the participants' job easier and more productive. This is not about making more work! If the solution includes new materials or equipment, have a discussion about how necessary they are to the solution.

2. Ask participants to complete Exercise 38.1. Ask them to share any ideas they have.

3. Provide a brief summary and answer any questions before wrapping up.

## Discussion Points

1. How can you be fair to your customers without giving away the shop?

2. How much time does it take to hand over a customer the right way? "Jane, this customer is calling about her invoice number 45980. It shows $95 instead of $63. Can you help, please?"

# EXERCISE 38.1: SUPER SERVICE ACTION PLAN

The actions I will take as a result of this activity are:

1. _____
   _____
   _____
   _____

2. _____
   _____
   _____
   _____

3. _____
   _____
   _____
   _____

4. _____
   _____
   _____
   _____

5. _____
   _____
   _____
   _____

6. _____
   _____
   _____

I will review this action plan on: _____  _____
                                         (date)                              (signed)

## Activity 39

# Helping Customers Be Profitable

## Background and Purpose

Every company wants to stress being profitable. This activity is about making the customers profitable. After all, if the customers are profitable, they will be in a better position to purchase from you.

Being profitable doesn't necessarily mean making more money. It can mean saving time or having the security of using a better product rather than an inferior one.

The purpose of this activity is to show participants how their product or service will help their customers be more profitable.

## Objectives

By the end of this activity, participants will be able to:

1. Understand the different kinds of profitability.

2. Understand how their product or service provides profitability to customers.

## Time

Approximately 1 hour

## Materials Required

1. Overhead 39.1

2. Exercises 39.2 and 39.3

## Mini Lecture

You are part of a business and it is your job to help the company grow profitable. Look at the two words, *profit* and *loss*. *Profit* has a healthy sound to it, while *loss* sounds like something terrible has happened.

If you can make your customers feel profitable, you will be providing a wonderful service. Profitability does not just mean making money. It has to do with saving time and people. A term used in the financial industry is "the time value of money." Money is more profitable if it is saved over time. For example, a dollar invested 20 years ago may have grown into $200 today. There is a value to time. Today we are going to look at how we can make our customers be profitable.

## Steps to Follow

1. Show Overhead 39.1. Explain that there are many different ways to be profitable. Ask participants to think about something they recently purchased. In what way did it make them more profitable?

2. Ask them to complete Exercise 39.2. Then ask them to form into groups of 4 or 5 and share their ideas. Ask the groups to come up with some ideas of their own. Ask each group to present its ideas to the whole group. (You can do this formally or informally, depending on the group.)

3. Ask participants to complete Exercise 39.3. If you have time, ask people to share their ideas.

4. Provide a brief summary and answer any questions before wrapping up.

# Ways to Be Profitable

1. Saving Time

2. Helping or Improving the Image

3. Providing Quality Service

4. Providing Guaranteed Service

5. Helping the Company to Stay in Business

6. Increasing Productivity

**EXERCISE 39.2**

Write a list of everything about you, your product, or your service that will help to make your customer profitable. Think in terms of saving time or money or people.

I help my customers to be profitable by:

1. _____

_____

2. _____

_____

3. _____

_____

4. _____

_____

5. _____

_____

6. _____

_____

7. _____

_____

8. _____

_____

# EXERCISE 39.3: SUPER SERVICE ACTION PLAN

The actions I will take as a result of this activity are:

1. _____

   _____

   _____

   _____

2. _____

   _____

   _____

   _____

3. _____

   _____

   _____

4. _____

   _____

   _____

5. _____

   _____

   _____

6. _____

   _____

   _____

I will review this action plan on: _____    _____
                                         (date)                              (signed)

## Background and Purpose

We only get out of life what we put into it. It's an old saying but it's still very true. The purpose of this workshop is to help participants understand that they are the most important aspect of customer service. They *are* part of the recipe; the question is, are they part of a recipe for disaster or a recipe for success?

## Objectives

By the end of this activity, participants will be able to:

1. Understand that they are "putting themselves into it."

2. Know the difference between "I can" and "I will."

## Time

Approximately 1 hour

## Materials Required

1. Overheads 40.1 and 40.2

2. Three glasses of water, 2 aspirin, 2 Bromo Seltzer tablets, 2 Alka Seltzer tablets, and one towel

3. Exercise 40.3

## Mini Lecture

Are you *with* the customers when you are with them, or are you just going through the motions? We often brush people off because they don't fit our image. It sounds harsh, but every time we dismiss people without finding out who they are, we are saying that they may as well not exist.

Super Service never stops! It's there with you all the time—in and out of the office, the department store, the agency, the salon. Wherever you work, Super Service is not something you can turn on and off at a whim.

# Activity 40
# Putting Yourself into It

Added value means going the extra mile or going beyond the call of duty.

A manager of a very large and well-known company that manufactures and sells soda recently said, "We're not a service company, we're a sales company!" Guess what? The two go hand in hand. At the end of every sale is a person, and every person wants Super Service.

## Steps to Follow

1. Show Overhead 40.1. Ask the participants what they think the difference is between the phrases "I can" and "I will." Explain that when we say, "I can," we are not saying that it will definitely happen. When we say, "I will," we are saying that it will be done and we are taking responsibility for doing it.

   For example, "I will send your request to…" instead of, "I can send your request to…." "I will talk to my manager," instead of, "I can talk to my manager." "I will get a service representative out tomorrow," instead of, "I can get a service representative out tomorrow."

2. Show Overhead 40.2. Explain that there are three types of people in customer service. The first type usually makes things happen. The second type watches things as they happen. The third type wonders what happened.

   Explain that Super Service types need to **make** things happen. Dramatize the key point by performing a simple demonstration with the glasses of water.

   **Demonstration:**

   Place the three glasses so that everyone can see them and fill them about three-quarters full of water. Place two aspirin in the first glass and wait for a response. Explain that this demonstrates one type of person. Place two Bromo Seltzer in the second glass. Notice that this employee often exhibits great bursts of enthusiasm, but quickly loses it and becomes like the first. Then place two Alka Seltzer tablets in the third glass. Notice that this type of employee produces a strong and stable output, and demonstrates the best way of "putting yourself in it!"

## Discussion Points

Ask these questions:

Which type of person would you rather be?

Is there a viable contribution that the different types can make?

How can we convert one type of individual into another type?

3. Hand out Exercise 40.3. Ask participants to complete it and invite those who are willing to share their thoughts.

4. Provide a brief summary and answer any questions before wrapping up.

# Phrases to Avoid
## "I can…"


# Phrases to Use
## "I will…"

# Three Types of People

- "Make it happen" type

- "Watch it happen" type

- "Wonder what happened" type

# EXERCISE 40.3: SUPER SERVICE ACTION PLAN

The actions I will take as a result of this activity are:

1. _____
   _____
   _____
   _____

2. _____
   _____
   _____
   _____

3. _____
   _____
   _____

4. _____
   _____
   _____

5. _____
   _____
   _____

6. _____
   _____
   _____

I will review this action plan on: _____    _____
                                        (date)                        (signed)

## Background and Purpose

Actions speak louder than words. We all know people we can depend on and those we cannot depend on—people who keep their word and those who do not. This activity stresses the importance of taking action. It explores why we sometimes think we cannot take action, and the steps to take in order to take the right action at the appropriate time.

## Objectives

By the end of this activity, participants will be able to:

1. Understand the importance of taking action.

2. Know when to take action and when not to take action.

3. Know how to keep from getting burned out.

## Time

Approximately 2 hours

## Materials Required

1. Overheads 41.1, 41.2, 41.3, and 41.4

3. Exercises 41.5, 41.6, and 41.7

## Mini Lecture

There is a difference between taking the right action and taking the wrong action. Taking the right action is easier when you come from a place of positive thoughts. Taking the wrong action is easier when you come from a place of negative thoughts.

If you have a lot of negative thoughts, your lives may take a negative turn of events. One way of getting rid of negative thoughts is to write them down and then burn the paper. Write a letter to someone who is troubling you, and then burn it. The fact that you got it out of your system is sometimes enough.

## Activity 41
# Take Action

Taking action not only helps you and the person you are helping; it leads you to enlightenment.

All action begins with a thought. If someone had not had the idea that candles are not the most effective source of light, electricity may never have been invented. Since everything begins with a thought, can we change the way we think? It is possible. It does take some effort, but it can be done.

## Steps to Follow

1. Show Overhead 41.1. Explain that sometimes we get burned out. We want to do a great job, but it doesn't work out the way we expected. Some of the reasons for this are: boredom, complexity, resources, money, and time. You can probably come up with a lot more reasons why projects don't get finished. However, the simple remedy is not to start something you cannot finish. Take a look at the project first. Can you manage it? Do you have too many things on your plate?

   If your boss asks you to take on more and you think it is impossible, say, "Does this project take priority over projects 3, 4, and 5? Or do you want me to finish those first?"

2. Show Overhead 41.2. Explain that words are like seeds. They scatter and fall all over your world. People hear them and learn what kind of person you are. Change your words and you will change your life. Instead of saying, "I can't do numbers," say, "I am getting better at numbers!" Pick out one or two of the negative phrases that you have used, and begin to use the positive affirmation instead.

3. Show Overhead 41.3. Explain that sometimes no action is better than taking action. Everything we do affects something else. That is the law of cause and effect. Sometimes the best action is to sit back and think about what effect your action will have. Will your action create something good or will it create something bad? Remember that "right thought comes before right action."

4. Show Overhead 41.4. Explain that these are sample criteria you can use to ensure that you are taking the right action. Ask if there are any other criteria that can be used. (If you have some examples of your own that have worked, you can also use those.)

5. Distribute Exercise 41.5. Have the participants form groups of 4 or 5. Ask them to read the problem and to come up with the right action to take. Ask each of the teams to present its solution. Be prepared to give feedback and to open the discussion to the rest of the group. Explain that if the supervisor is approachable it may be wise to talk to them about the need for Customer Service training on Right Attitude. You are stating the problem without pointing a finger.

6. Distribute Exercise 41.6. Ask participants to complete it and answer any questions they may have as a result of this exercise.

7. Hand out Exercise 41.7 and ask participants to complete it.

8. Provide a brief summary and answer any questions before wrapping up.

# Why Action Stops

1. Boredom: The project loses its sparkle.

2. Complexity: It's harder than we thought.

3. Resources: People or equipment are limited.

4. Money: We've run out of cash.

5. Time: It's taking too long.

# Phrases to Use

| **Instead of...** | **Use...** |
| --- | --- |
| I hate myself. | I love myself. |
| I'm bored. | I am content. |
| It will never happen. | It will happen. |
| Nothing works. | Everything works. |
| I never get what I want. | I get everything I want. |
| My life is horrible. | My life is great. |
| My customers are all difficult. | My customers are great. |
| I can't find happiness. | I am happy. |
| I am not fulfilled. | I am fulfilled. |

# The Best Action
# May Be No Action...

# ...Right Thought
# Comes Before
# Right Action

# Criteria for Taking Action

- Is it wise?

- Will it solve the problem?

- Will it create more problems?

- Can it be done?

- How do I go about it?

- What specific action will I take?

# EXERCISE 41.5: TAKING RIGHT ACTION

Please read this situation. You and your team should discuss the situation and come up with the right action for this person to take. You should have valid reasons for your decision and be prepared to discuss your reasons with the rest of the group.

*Situation:*

You are a new employee (one month) with the company and are working in customer service, a department with 60 people and 5 supervisors. A friend of your parents (who is head of the customer service department) got you the job.

You notice that your supervisor has a really bad attitude about the customers. It's not something you can put your finger on exactly, but you know the customers feel it. It's a superior attitude, as if the customers should be grateful for any type of service they receive. Last week, two customers complained to you about the supervisor. You do not know what to do about the situation. You don't like to work in this atmosphere. Should you:

a.  Tell your parents?

b.  Tell the supervisor?

c.  Tell your parents' friend (the head of the department)?

d.  Ignore the problem and hope it will go away?

e.  Come up with a completely different solution?

# EXERCISE 41.6

Please write down (in 15 words or fewer) a current situation, problem, or issue that you need to resolve.

_____

_____

_____

Now write down the right action you need to take. Use these criteria for judging your right action:

Is it wise? _____

Will it solve the problem? _____

Will it create more problems? _____

Can it be done? _____

How do I go about it?_____

What specific action will I take? _____

_____

_____

_____

_____

# EXERCISE 41.7: SUPER SERVICE ACTION PLAN

The actions I will take as a result of this activity are:

1. _____

_____

_____

_____

2. _____

_____

_____

_____

3. _____

_____

_____

_____

4. _____

_____

_____

_____

5. _____

_____

_____

_____

6. _____

_____

_____

I will review this action plan on: _____     _____
                                          (date)                                   (signed)

## Background and Purpose

Actions speak louder than words: If we say one thing and do another, guess what the customer remembers? It doesn't matter if we have a million great excuses, nobody wants to hear excuses—especially customers—they want the job done. The purpose of this workshop is to help people understand that customers judge on behavior, not on words. It is about saying what we will do, and then doing what we said we would do.

## Objectives

By the end of this activity, participants will be able to:

1. Understand the importance of behavior.

2. Know how to follow through on what is said.

## Time

Approximately 20 minutes

## Materials Required

1. Overheads 42.1 and 42.2

2. Exercises 42.3 and 42.4

## Activity 42
# Behavior Is What Customers Remember

To serve others is ultimately to serve ourselves, because when we open our hearts, our spirit grows and becomes stronger.

## Mini Lecture

If you have listened to your customers and identified their needs, you are ready to carry out an action plan. This means taking action to ensure the right steps are taken, by the right people, as quickly as possible. Simply stated, it means doing what you said you would do!

You will need to follow up with your customers to keep them informed of any progress or delays. Many customers complain about a lack of communication between departments or employees, particularly in large organizations.

The way to reduce this cause of friction is to make sure you let the right people know what they need to know. Keeping people informed before something happens is much easier than telling them after the event.

Often, the small tasks that we put off create the most problems, like answering our messages. We're tired; we don't want to return calls. We put them off until later, but it doesn't get any easier—it just gets later.

## Steps to Follow

1. Show Overhead 42.1. Explain that good behavior can be learned. It doesn't take any special intelligence to display good behavior. It also doesn't mean losing our individuality; it just means respecting ourselves, our environment, and our space.

2. Show Overhead 42.2. Explain that creating a pattern of good behavior is simple if we follow these steps. If you have a personal anecdote to highlight any of the steps, please use it. For example, "I once had a shipment that was delayed by three weeks. I told the customers immediately and they were able to change all their training class dates. Later they thanked me for keeping them in the loop."

3. Hand out Exercise 42.3 and ask participants to complete it. Emphasize that they are doing the exercise from the customer's point of view. Determine by a show of hands the one item they ranked as the most important. Make a note of the most important items, and discuss as a group why they are the most important.

4. Distribute Exercise 42.4 and ask participants to complete it. Ask for any feedback on their ideas.

5. Provide a brief summary and answer any questions before wrapping up.

# Steps for Good Behavior

1. Respond to messages as soon as you get them.

2. Leave a place better than you found it.

3. Put things back where you found them.

4. Keep people informed of any changes that affect them.

# Communicating Good Behavior

**1. Give regular updates and progress reports.**
   *Let customers know what is going on so they are prepared.*

**2. Communicate delays promptly.**
   *If customers know about delays, they can make changes in their schedules.*

**3. State exactly what was done.**
   *Explain what was done and what steps you have taken.*

**4. Give a personal reassurance to the customer.**
   *Tell the customer that you have solved the problem.*

**5. Help your customer be proactive.**
   *Provide information about preventive maintenance.*

**6. Thank your customer.**
   *The customer has made an effort to bring the issue to your attention. It is better to know what is not working than to have people take their business to the competition.*

## EXERCISE 42.3: BEHAVIOR STEPS

**Directions:** Rank the following items by circling a number from 1 to 10 (10 = highest, 1 = lowest) according to what is important in your experience as a customer. In other words, what keeps you going back?

| | | | | | | | | | | |
|---|---|---|---|---|---|---|---|---|---|---|
| Messages Responded to Quickly | 1 | 2 | 3 | 4 | 5 | 6 | 7 | 8 | 9 | 10 |
| Open Communication | 1 | 2 | 3 | 4 | 5 | 6 | 7 | 8 | 9 | 10 |
| Delays Communicated Promptly | 1 | 2 | 3 | 4 | 5 | 6 | 7 | 8 | 9 | 10 |
| Kept Up to Date on the Situation | 1 | 2 | 3 | 4 | 5 | 6 | 7 | 8 | 9 | 10 |
| Personal Reassurance | 1 | 2 | 3 | 4 | 5 | 6 | 7 | 8 | 9 | 10 |
| Ability to Be Proactive | 1 | 2 | 3 | 4 | 5 | 6 | 7 | 8 | 9 | 10 |
| Being Thanked | 1 | 2 | 3 | 4 | 5 | 6 | 7 | 8 | 9 | 10 |
| Regular Progress Reports | 1 | 2 | 3 | 4 | 5 | 6 | 7 | 8 | 9 | 10 |
| Great Presentation | 1 | 2 | 3 | 4 | 5 | 6 | 7 | 8 | 9 | 10 |
| Great Follow-Through | 1 | 2 | 3 | 4 | 5 | 6 | 7 | 8 | 9 | 10 |

Now underline the top item that you ranked the most important to a customer.

# EXERCISE 42.4: SUPER SERVICE ACTION PLAN

The actions I will take as a result of this activity are:

1. _____
   _____
   _____
   _____

2. _____
   _____
   _____
   _____

3. _____
   _____
   _____
   _____

4. _____
   _____
   _____
   _____

5. _____
   _____
   _____
   _____

6. _____
   _____
   _____

I will review this action plan on: _____    _____
                                          (date)                        (signed)

# Activity 43

# When the Company Is Used as an Excuse for Bad Action

You can foresee stress.
You can foresee burnout.
You can plan how to handle them.

## Background and Purpose

Sometimes it seems easier to blame the company for a problem, but when customers hear phrases like "I wish they would get their act together in accounting," or "We've had problems like this in the past," it does not inspire confidence.

The purpose of this activity is to allow the participants to take responsibility for their own actions or problems. It also allows them to use a team brainstorming activity to find solutions to any current problems they may be having.

## Objectives

By the end of this activity, participants will be able to:

1. Know phrases to use and those to avoid.

2. Follow guidelines for follow-up action.

3. Accept responsibility for getting the job done.

4. Find solutions to current problems.

## Time

Approximately 2 hours

## Materials Required

1. Overheads 43.1 and 43.2

2. A large variety of colored pens, crayons and blank sheets of paper for drawing on. (You can also use Play-Doh™ or Lego™ for this exercise.)

3. Exercises 43.3 and 43.4

## Mini Lecture

While it might get it off your chest to blame the company for a problem, it doesn't do anybody any good. It doesn't help you, the customer, or the company. It's not to say that the company doesn't make mistakes...but does it help the customer to know that? If a problem is recurring within the company, then it is your job to either find a solution, or let the right people know about the problem. Don't do that in a complaining way, but by saying "I've noticed this problem happening a lot recently and I think we could solve it by doing this" or, "This is a recurring problem and I need help finding a solution."

## Steps to Follow

1. Show Overheads 43.1 and 43.2. Explain that there are some commonly used phrases that should be avoided, and some that can be used. Ask the group if they have any examples of phrases they have found to work.

2. Ask participants to individually sketch out a picture of how they "see" one of the main problems of their job. Ask them to be creative. For example, they can use sports, TV shows, or movies, such as a robo-cop with all the wires sticking out, or *Speed,* with a bus hurtling out of control. (You can use Play-Doh™ or Lego™ to create a structure if you prefer.)

   Divide participants into groups of 3 or 4. Ask participants to share their pictures with the group and explain the problems. Give the groups 30 minutes to find a workable solution for each problem.

   Ask each group to present its problems and solutions. (If they have time, they can draw the illustrations on a flip chart.)

   **Discussion questions:**

   How do you see your problems?

   How would your customers see the problem?

   What solutions have you found?

   What new action will you take?

3. Distribute Exercise 43.3 and ask participants to complete it. Ask for feedback and lead a class discussion based on the personal action steps.

4. Ask participants to complete Exercise 43.4.

5. Provide a brief summary and answer any questions before wrapping up.

# Phrases to Avoid

"It's usually an operator problem
and not the product!"

"I don't understand why you are still frustrated.
I thought the problem was solved."

"Have they been able to sort out
your problem yet?"

# Phrases to Use

"Let me make sure I have the right number:
6587; is that correct?"

"I'm adding your name to our database, so we can
contact you when our new enhancements come out.
Is that okay?"

"It was a pleasure working with you. Thank you for
bringing this problem to our attention."

"Your account has been credited."

"Your system is now working correctly."

"Does this meet your needs?"

**EXERCISE 43.3**

Think about all the ways you can improve the way you solve problems. Add your own personal action steps at the end of the list:

1.  Take initiative.

2.  Be responsible.

3.  Be willing to make decisions.

4.  Use "right thinking" before acting.

5.  Get input from the customer.

6.  Listen for clues as to how the customer is feeling.

7.  Develop a clear mental picture of the situation.

8.  Keep your tone quiet and peaceful.

9.  Develop a desire to serve.

10. Clarify, verify, and check for mutual agreement on problems.

11. Communicate delays promptly.

12. Explain the action plan.

13. Thank the customer.

14. Complete the action plan within the stated time frame.

15. _____

16. _____

17. _____

18. _____

19. _____

20. _____

# EXERCISE 43.4: SUPER SERVICE ACTION PLAN

The actions I will take as a result of this activity are:

1. _____

   _____

   _____

   _____

2. _____

   _____

   _____

   _____

3. _____

   _____

   _____

   _____

4. _____

   _____

   _____

   _____

5. _____

   _____

   _____

   _____

6. _____

   _____

   _____

   _____

I will review this action plan on: _____    _____
                                        (date)                        (signed)

## Background and Purpose

There are times to uncover the problem, and there are times to uncover the satisfaction. After all, a product or service is designed to provide satisfaction rather than problems. But do customer service providers really use this powerful tool?

The purpose of this workshop is to help the participants build on satisfaction, by searching for more possibilities of satisfaction.

## Objectives

By the end of this activity, participants will be able to:

1. Understand how to build on satisfaction.

2. Improve customer interactions by building on satisfaction.

## Time

Approximately 2 hours

## Materials Required

1. Exercise 44.1

2. Overhead 44.2

3. Flip chart and markers

4. Exercise 44.3

## Mini Lecture

One psychiatrist always asks patients this question: "Tell me about a time when everything worked really well for you." Together, they then build on what worked well. This can work with our customers; we can build on satisfaction just as easily as we can build on problems. It does not mean that we ignore problems, or that when a customer has a problem we stop probing and asking questions about the problem.

# Activity 44
# Build on Satisfaction

Added value means going the extra mile or going beyond the call of duty.

Building on satisfaction is part of problem solving. For example, a telephone system designed for three phone outlets causes frustration if there are five people wanting to use the phone at the same time. If a customer calls with a problem on one of the telephones and that problem is fixed, it still does not solve the overall problem: There aren't enough units to handle the calls.

Building on satisfaction means looking for more than solutions or problems; it means finding out what works and building on that.

## Steps to Follow

1. Distribute Exercise 44.1. Ask participants to work alone and identify as many legitimate words as they can from the letters available to them in the word *customer*. Explain that they must first make two predictions: The number of words they will *individually* identify, and the word score of the *highest producer*. Give them 5 minutes and set them loose on the task.

2. Show Overhead 44.2, listing all of the possibilities. Tell them there are 45 possible words. Beginning with the highest number, 45, count down, asking people to raise their hands when you reach their own individual score.

   **Discussion Questions:**

   How many words did you predict you would find? How does your prediction compare with how you actually did?

   Did anyone predict the correct highest producer's score?

   Did you exceed your expectations or fall short?

   What does this exercise illustrate to you? (There is always a lot more to be found than we think possible.)

   In what ways could we search for greater satisfaction in our customers?

3. Have participants break into groups of 4 to 5. Ask the groups to brainstorm as many ideas as they can think of that will help build satisfaction in their jobs. Allow 5 to 10 minutes. Start with one group and ask them to share their ideas. Write down the key concepts on a flip chart. Continue with the other groups until you have all the ideas. Discuss the ideas with the group.

   **Discussion Questions:**

   How many of these ideas can you use?

   Do any of them require substantial changes?

   How easy will they be to adapt?

4. Ask participants to complete Exercise 44.3. If you have time, ask for feedback on this exercise. Use examples to begin a discussion with the group.

5. Provide a brief summary and answer any questions before wrapping up.

# EXERCISE 44.1: CUSTOMER POSSIBILITIES

In the space below, write down as many words as possible using the letters available in the word *Customer.*

Before you begin, make two predictions: The number of words you expect to identify *as an individual,* and the number of words the *highest producer* will identify.

I will identify _____ words.

The highest producer will identify _____ words.

# Customer Possibilities

| | | |
|---|---|---|
| Come | Emu | Rut |
| Comer | Me | Set |
| Comes | Met | Some |
| Core | More | Sore |
| Corset | Most | Sum |
| Cost | Mouse | To |
| Costume | Must | Toes |
| Costumer | Or | Tome |
| Cot | Ore | Tomes |
| Cote | Ort | Tore |
| Course | Rest | Tour |
| Court | Rome | True |
| Cur | Rose | Us |
| Custom | Rot | Use |
| Cut | Rote | User |

# EXERCISE 44.3: SUPER SERVICE ACTION PLAN

The actions I will take as a result of this activity are:

1. _____
   _____
   _____
   _____

2. _____
   _____
   _____
   _____

3. _____
   _____
   _____
   _____

4. _____
   _____
   _____
   _____

5. _____
   _____
   _____
   _____

6. _____
   _____
   _____

I will review this action plan on: _____     _____
                                        (date)                              (signed)

## Background and Purpose

Most people don't do things unless they feel there is some benefit in doing it. At work, the benefits are not always so obvious. It is not always obvious, for example, that the person who benefits most from Super Service is the person providing the service.

The purpose of this activity is to build awareness of the benefits of providing Super Service.

## Objective

By the end of this activity, participants will be able to:

- Identify the benefits of delivering Super Service.

## Time

Approximately 20 minutes

## Materials Required

1. Overhead 45.1
2. Flip chart and markers
3. Exercise 45.2

## Mini Lecture

Most people think that the person who benefits most from Super Service is the customer, but that is not the case. The person who benefits most from delivering Super Service is the person delivering it. How do we know this? Because the person who gives is the person who experiences the power of giving.

(Please share any personal experience of the benefits of giving Super Service.)

## Activity 45
# Who Benefits?

When you explain to customers *how* their service needs will be met by your organization, they feel in control.

## Steps to Follow

1. Show Overhead 45.1. Explain that *The Wall Street Journal* published this Workforce Study, and that most people rank open communication as the number one job factor.

2. Ask people to pair up with a partner. Together they will make a list of the benefits of delivering service. Allow 10 minutes for pairs to develop their lists.

3. Ask each pair to decide which of the benefits they discussed is the most important. Ask each pair to share the top ranking benefit with the rest of the group.

   **Discussion Questions:**

   Why did you rank this as the top benefit?

   What does it give you?

   What does it give your customer?

   Is it something that happens naturally, or is it the result of a thought-out process?

4. Distribute Exercise 45.2 and ask participants to complete it.

5. Provide a brief summary and answer any questions before wrapping up.

# Important Job Factors

| | Rank (1 = highest 10 = lowest) |
|---|:---:|
| Advancement opportunity | 8 |
| Control over work content | 3 |
| Flexible work schedule | 7 |
| Fringe benefits | 6 |
| Job security | 4 |
| Nature of work | 2 |
| Open communication | 1 |
| Salary or wages | 9 |
| Size of organization | 10 |
| Stimulating work | 5 |

# EXERCISE 45.2: SUPER SERVICE ACTION PLAN

The actions I will take as a result of this activity are:

1. _____

_____

_____

_____

2. _____

_____

_____

_____

3. _____

_____

_____

4. _____

_____

_____

5. _____

_____

_____

6. _____

_____

_____

I will review this action plan on: _____     _____
                              (date)                                    (signed)

## Activity 46
# Be Helpful

## Background and Purpose

Being helpful is one of the most important aspects of delivering Super Service. But what does it mean? If you want your customer service providers to be helpful, what do they need to be doing that they are not doing already?

The purpose of this activity is to identify what is helpful and what is unhelpful.

## Objectives

By the end of this activity, participants will be able to:

1.  Come to consensus about what is helpful and what is unhelpful.

2.  Identify areas where they can be helpful.

## Time

Approximately 45 minutes

## Materials Required

1.  Flip chart and marker pens

2.  Exercise 46.1

## Mini Lecture

Being helpful is not something that is taught at school. It is something we perceive others doing; we experience being helped. Just as important, however, we perceive others being unhelpful, and we certainly feel it when people are unhelpful toward us.

It doesn't take very much to be helpful. You can decide how much you want to help, or how little. It can depend on how much time you have available to help, but more often than not, being helpful is an attitude of mind. Some people seem to be born with a natural amount of helpfulness. However, it can be learned and practiced until it becomes a habit. We want to develop the seeds of being helpful until it becomes a natural habit.

## Steps to Follow

1. Ask the group to brainstorm all the ways they can be unhelpful. Write them down on a flip chart. When they are finished, underline each unhelpful possibility that is related to attitude. Explain that most unhelpful acts begin with having an unhelpful attitude.

   **Discussion Questions**

   How does it affect us when we are unhelpful?

   How does it affect the environment?

2. Ask the group to brainstorm all the ways they can be helpful. Again, underline all the possibilities related to attitude.

   **Discussion Questions**

   How many of these helpful ideas are time-related?

   How much time do they really take?

   How can we incorporate being helpful into the work environment, with our internal customers and with our external customers?

3. Distribute Exercise 46.1 and ask participants to complete it.

4. Provide a brief summary and answer any questions before wrapping up.

# EXERCISE 46.1: SUPER SERVICE ACTION PLAN

The actions I will take as a result of this activity are:

1. _____

   _____

   _____

   _____


2. _____

   _____

   _____

   _____


3. _____

   _____

   _____

   _____


4. _____

   _____

   _____

   _____


5. _____

   _____

   _____

   _____


6. _____

   _____

   _____

   _____


I will review this action plan on: _____        _____

(date)                                                       (signed)

# Activity 47
# On the Front Line

## Background and Purpose

If customers have problems, the first person they talk with is a customer service provider. Customer Service providers are on the front line of communication.

The purpose of this activity is to help customer service providers understand that they are on the front line, what it means, and how they can use that position to the best advantage.

## Objective

By the end of this activity, participants will be able to:

- Develop front line tactics for providing customer satisfaction.

## Time

Approximately 2 hours

## Materials Required

1. Overheads 47.1 and 47.2

2. Exercises 47.3 and 47.4

## Mini Lecture

You are at the front line, the liaison between your customer and your company. When you take responsibility for this role, your life will become easier. You are at the front line; you are the first point of contact for your customers. Your attitude and your way of taking responsibility will affect your customer's attitude.

Ask what level of service participants receive when they are customers. Find out what was good or bad about their experiences. Elicit feedback on the examples. Ask how the companies involved compare with the participants' own organizations.

One of the key components of selling is having great energy.

## Steps to Follow

1. Show Overhead 47.1. Explain that positive front-line service can be created by dealing with problems quickly, by showing concern for other people, and by providing an unexpected high level of service. Customers are disappointed when they are promised a delivery at 11 a.m. and it doesn't arrive until 1 p.m.

2. Divide participants into teams of 3 to 5 and ask each team to elect a spokesperson. Ask each team to consider how a local bank can give customers a positive front-line experience. Allow 10 to 15 minutes. Then take feedback from the spokespeople.

   Show Overhead 47.2 to help with answers. Ask, How many of these items could the customer service provider take responsibility for?

3. Distribute Exercise 47.3 and divide participants into different teams of 3 to 5 to answer the questions. Ask each team to elect a spokesperson. Allow 20 to 25 minutes for this exercise. Then take feedback from each team. Ensure that agreement is reached on areas for improvement.

4. Distribute Exercise 47.4 and ask participants to decide what they are personally going to do differently as a result of the activity. Ask them to complete their own personal action plans.

5. Provide a brief summary of key points and answer any questions before wrapping up.

## Front-Line Tactics That Work

1. Deal with problems quickly.

2. Show concern.

3. Provide a high level of service.

4. Have a helpful attitude.

5. Underpromise rather than overpromise.

# A Positive Front-Line Experience

1. Layout is user friendly, with clear directions.

2. Floor and counters are clean.

3. Teller's name is visible.

4. Informational pamphlets are visible.

5. Pens are available and working.

6. Service is immediate.

7. Service is good despite the wait. (An apology is made if you wait more than five minutes.)

8. Teller establishes eye contact.

9. Teller greets you.

10. Teller is properly dressed.

11. Teller calls you by name.

12. Teller thanks you or says goodbye at the end of the transaction.

**EXERCISE 47.3**

1. Who are your customers?

2. What point of contact do your customers have with you?

3. What do your customers expect of you?

4. In which areas are you meeting customer expectations?

5. In which areas are customer expectations not being met?

6. How can these areas be improved?

# EXERCISE 47.4: SUPER SERVICE ACTION PLAN

The actions I will take as a result of this activity are:

1. _____

   _____

   _____

   _____

2. _____

   _____

   _____

   _____

3. _____

   _____

   _____

   _____

4. _____

   _____

   _____

   _____

5. _____

   _____

   _____

6. _____

   _____

   _____

I will review this action plan on: _____    _____
                                        (date)                              (signed)

# Activity 48
# Promises, Promises

## Background and Purpose

Being customer-oriented is fine, but sometimes people overpromise and underperform. This gives the customer a false set of expectations of yourself and your company.

The purpose of this activity is to enable participants to give customers a level of service that matches their expectations.

## Objectives

By the end of this activity, participants will be able to:

1. Assess what customers think of the current service level.

2. Plan how to enhance customer service today, in areas that do not require authority from management.

3. Plan how to enhance customer service in areas that do require authority from management.

## Time

Approximately 2 hours

## Materials Required

1. Flip charts and markers (including one for each group)

2. Tape for hanging the flip chart sheets on the wall

3. Overhead 48.1

4. Checklist 48.2

5. Exercise 48.3

## Mini Lecture

Explain that providing customer satisfaction is like a journey: You need to know which direction to travel in and this requires two points on the map, where you are now and where you want to go in the future. If a customer is experiencing satisfaction or dissatisfaction, we need to know. If they are satisfied, how do we exceed their expectations? If they are dissatisfied, how do we move them toward satisfaction?

## Steps to Follow

1. Write the heading **Satisfied** on the flip chart. Explain that there are various degrees of satisfaction. Some customers are very satisfied, and some customers are just satisfied. Ask the group to provide examples of why their customers would be satisfied. Write all the examples down under the Satisfied heading.

   Answers to look for:

   *Delivery of basic offering*

   *Common courtesy*

   *Good reaction to customer's viewpoint*

   *Someone going out of the way to solve a problem*

   *Simplify complicated arrangements or instructions*

   *Do something special for the customer*

   Ask them to tell you which examples their customers are now experiencing, and put an asterisk next to those examples.

2. Next write the heading **Dissatisfied**. Ask the group to provide examples of why their customers would be dissatisfied. Write all the examples down under this heading.

   Answers to look for:

   *Failure to deliver the basic offering*

   *Failure to provide common courtesy*

   *Failure to acknowledge customer's point of view*

   Ask them to tell you which examples their customers are now experiencing, and put an asterisk next to those examples.

3. Show Overhead 48.1. Explain that there are different types of transactions that can make customers feel more or less satisfied with a particular product or service. Ask them if they have experienced a positive event that went sour? How to enhance a nonevent? How to turn a negative experience around?

   Answers to look for:

   *It is easy to build on personal satisfaction. It is also easy for customers to become quickly dissatisfied (if the car is scratched, for example).*

   *The nonevent has to be enhanced to make a mundane experience a pleasant one.*

   *The unpleasant experience requires that customers be reassured and the company's reputation rebuilt.*

4. Distribute Checklist 48.2 and ask participants to complete it as individuals. When they are finished, tell them they can refer to this checklist in the next group exercise.

5. Divide participants into groups by similar job type or function. Ask them to put themselves in their customers' shoes and make a list of all the things that are satisfying and dissatisfying to them. (They can include items highlighted earlier by the group.)

   Now ask them to provide solutions and enhancements to everything on that list. Ask them to put everything that requires management approval under one heading and everything they can now implement under another heading.

   Tell the groups to prepare a group presentation. Allow 30 minutes for this exercise.

6. Give each group 5 to 10 minutes to present its findings. At the end of the presentations, discuss the findings and give feedback.

7. Distribute Exercise 48.3. Ask participants to complete it individually. However, if there are participants from one section or department, it may be preferable for them to complete a joint Recommendations Plan.

   Note to facilitator: If you are also in a consulting role, you may want to make a note of all the solutions and enhancements that need management approval and ensure that a meeting is set up to discuss them.

8. Provide a brief summary and answer any questions before wrapping up.

# Types of Transactions

- **Feeling positive—exciting—buying a new car**

- **Nonevent—not exciting—buying a lightbulb**

- **Feeling negative—returning faulty goods**

# CHECKLIST 48.2

Put yourself in your customer's shoes. As one of your customers, would you make the following statements? Put an "x" in the appropriate boxes.

|  | True | False |
|---|---|---|
| The employees are welcoming and look clean and neat. | ❑ | ❑ |
| The environment is comfortable, clean, and tidy. | ❑ | ❑ |
| Everyone looks like they enjoy their job. | ❑ | ❑ |
| Everyone seems pleased I've called (even if I have a problem). | ❑ | ❑ |
| If they make a promise, it's guaranteed they will keep it. | ❑ | ❑ |
| If they make a mistake, they are the first to admit it. | ❑ | ❑ |
| If I'm angry when I start out, I always end up feeling better. | ❑ | ❑ |
| When I complain, they are so helpful that I almost feel guilty. | ❑ | ❑ |
| When a problem arises, they always take ownership of it. | ❑ | ❑ |
| They are so efficient, I could learn a thing or two. | ❑ | ❑ |
| It's not so much what they do; they have a great attitude. | ❑ | ❑ |

# EXERCISE 48.3: SUPER SERVICE ACTION PLAN

The actions I will take as a result of this activity are:

1. _____

   _____

   _____

   _____

2. _____

   _____

   _____

   _____

3. _____

   _____

   _____

4. _____

   _____

   _____

5. _____

   _____

   _____

6. _____

   _____

   _____

I will review this action plan on: _____    _____
                                               (date)                                         (signed)

# Activity 49
# How to Handle an Unhappy Customer

It doesn't matter whether customers are right or wrong.
They need to air their complaints.

## Background and Purpose

Every company wants to have happy customers; however, this is not always possible. Even happy customers can easily become unhappy customers. Knowing how to handle the unhappy customer is a key to providing excellent customer service.

The purpose of this activity is to provide tools for handling an unhappy customer.

## Objective

By the end of this activity, participants will be able to:

■ Handle an unhappy customer.

## Time

Approximately 45 minutes

## Materials Required

1. Overhead 49.1

2. Exercises 49.2 and 49.3

## Mini Lecture

It is important to know that a happy customer can easily become an unhappy customer. Being put on hold too long or misinterpreting a tone of voice can change the customer's emotional state. For example, if a customer calls to check on an account status and you have just handled a difficult customer, you may still have tension in your voice.

## Steps to Follow

1. Show Overhead 49.1. Explain that you can think of customers in terms of traffic lights. The happy customer is like a green light—everything is go. We may take advantage of these customers because we feel more at ease with them. The neu-

tral customer is like a yellow light—you should proceed with caution. Everything may seem fine, but there could be something unexpected coming at any minute. The unhappy customer is like a red light—you should definitely stop and think about what action to take.

2. Divide the group into teams and provide them with Exercise 49.2. Ask them to decide which is the best way to handle each of the customer situations. Discuss their answers with the class.

   Answers to Look For

   *"I have always used this product or service, and I have never had any problems." This is a happy customer. You want to keep this customer happy without looking for problems. Possible response: "I'm very glad to hear that and we want to keep it that way. My name is _____. Please feel free to call if we can be of any further assistance."*

   "I don't usually complain. In fact I could be wrong. I may have been oversold on this product. Do I really need all the bells and whistles?" This is a neutral customer. You want to make sure he or she feels listened to and resolve the issues. Possible response: "May I ask you a couple of questions to see if this is the right product for you or not? Sometimes a product may seem to have more than you need, but it's the only one that has all of what you do need."

   "Why do you bother to advertise customer satisfaction on the TV? It's a joke! I have not experienced one ounce of satisfaction since I came into this store." This is an unhappy customer. You want to move this customer toward being neutral or happy by letting him or her vent and by listening. Possible response: "I'm sorry that you have had a bad experience. I would like to do my best to change your experience. How may I help you?"

3. Distribute Exercise 49.3 and ask participants to complete it as individuals. If you have time, discuss some of their ideas.

4. Provide a brief summary and answer any questions before wrapping up.

# Customers Are Like Traffic Lights

Happy = Green = Go
Neutral = Yellow = Caution
Unhappy = Red = Stop

**EXERCISE 49.2**

Here are three statements that could be made by any customer. Decide as a team what type of customer would say it, which is the best response and why.

1. "I have always used this product or service, and I have never had any problems."

2. "I don't usually complain. In fact I could be wrong. I may have been oversold on this product. Do I really need all the 'bells and whistles?'"

3. "Why do you bother to advertise customer satisfaction on the TV? It's a joke! I have not experienced one ounce of satisfaction since I came into this store."

# EXERCISE 49.3: SUPER SERVICE ACTION PLAN

The actions I will take as a result of this activity are:

1. _____
   _____
   _____
   _____

2. _____
   _____
   _____
   _____

3. _____
   _____
   _____

4. _____
   _____
   _____

5. _____
   _____
   _____

6. _____
   _____
   _____

I will review this action plan on: _____     _____
                                   (date)                          (signed)

## Activity 50

# How to Defuse Unhappy Customers

Seeing the good in yourself and your circumstances is an important step in developing a positive attitude.

## Background and Purpose

When customers are all fired up and angry, they don't have time to be friendly. In those cases, the service provider has to assume the entire responsibility.

The purpose of this activity is to provide ten keys for defusing an unhappy customer.

## Objectives

By the end of this activity, participants will be able to:

- Use the ten keys for defusing an unhappy customer.

## Time

Approximately 35 minutes

## Materials Required

1. Overhead 50.1
2. Flip chart and markers
3. Exercise 50.2

## Mini Lecture

An unhappy customer is like a stone in your shoe. If you take it out immediately, the problem is solved. If you leave the stone in, the pain gradually increases and creates problems in other parts of your body. The longer a customer is unhappy, the more he or she becomes aggravated and the scale of the unhappiness escalates.

When you listen to a problem, you own it. That means you cannot pass it on to someone else. It is your responsibility, your problem, and you must find the solution.

A key factor in handling an unhappy customer is attitude. Your attitude is contagious. If you hold a friendly space for customers to vent their anger, they will calm down more quickly, and you will feel more in control and professional.

So fight fire with friendliness. This does not mean to act as if the customer does not have a problem, or not to give the problem the attention it deserves. It means that you detach from the problem, you solve it, and you remain friendly.

## Steps to Follow

Show Overhead 50.1. Read the ten keys for defusing unhappy customers. Explain that a key skill when dealing with an unhappy customer is the ability to empathize. This does not mean agreeing immediately that you are wrong, but sympathizing and acknowledging the customer's emotions. One of the keys to empathy is treating other people as you would like to be treated.

1. Divide participants into teams of 3 to 5 and ask the groups to brainstorm a list of the most common types of unhappy customer scenarios. Instruct each team to explain how they would normally handle these scenarios and, if necessary, to devise new ways of handling the scenarios (based on the ten keys).

2. Bring the teams back together again as one group. Ask participants for examples of solutions and discuss whether there are any areas of product knowledge or company policy that remain unclear. Clarify these points with the rest of the participants. Record responses on a flip chart.

3. Distribute Exercise 50.2 and ask participants to complete it individually. Ask for any ideas or feedback.

4. Briefly summarize the key points and answer any questions before wrapping up.

# Ten Keys for Defusing Unhappy Customers

1. Show empathy—*"I'm sorry."*

2. Encourage venting—*"Please tell me what happened."*

3. Stay objectives—*"I understand how you would feel that way."*

4. Remain calm—*"I believe we can resolve this."*

5. Listen attentively—*"Aha, yes. I see."*

6. Take responsibility—*"I will make sure the problem is resolved."*

7. Involve the customer—*"How would you like to see this handled?"*

8. Give added value—*"Another way we can resolve the situation is…"*

9. Provide an action plan—*"This is what I propose to do…"*

10. Involve your manager—*"I will let management know of this problem."*

# EXERCISE 50.2: SUPER SERVICE ACTION PLAN

The actions I will take as a result of this activity are:

1. _____

   _____

   _____

   _____

2. _____

   _____

   _____

   _____

3. _____

   _____

   _____

   _____

4. _____

   _____

   _____

   _____

5. _____

   _____

   _____

6. _____

   _____

   _____

I will review this action plan on: _____  _____
                                        (date)                        (signed)

## Background and Purpose

Often a customer just needs to get something off his or her chest. The very fact of being able to vent is enough; customers just need a place to do it.

The purpose of this activity is to help customer service providers understand venting. It is not personal, anyone else would receive the same treatment, and while it may be uncomfortable at the time, after customers have vented, they often become quite remorseful.

## Objectives

By the end of this activity, participants will be able to:

1. Understand the purpose of venting.

2. Use some key steps with a venting customer.

## Time

Approximately 1 hour and 30 minutes

## Materials Required

1. Overheads 51.1 and 51.2

2. Exercises 51.3, 51.4, and 51.5

## Mini Lecture

It doesn't matter if customers are right or wrong; they need to air their complaints. If you do not treat them with care, you may lose them altogether. It is like whitewater rafting. Your customer is the raging water, and you are taking great care to steer your raft to calmer waters. You do not allow yourself to get sucked in. The customer's words flow like the water underneath you. Your breathing is calm, and on every exhalation you let go of your own emotions.

One of the main problems when people are venting is that we get sucked in.

# Activity 51
# Venting

When that happens, we become part of the problem. All customers see then is their anger reflected back to them, so it is very important to remain calm.

The main way to remain calm is to listen. Act like a sounding board. Listen for the problem and let all the other emotional words bounce off you.

## Steps to Follow

1. Show Overhead 51.1. Explain that you should never do certain things when a customer is venting. Say: Think about the last time you were angry. What would have happened if someone had told you to calm down? It is like a red rag to a bull—it often does the opposite. If someone interrupts you when you are angry and venting, how does that feel? If you are angry and the other person ignores your anger, how does that feel?

2. Show Overhead 51.2. Ask the participants: Have you ever experienced a venting customer? Did they use any of these techniques? What worked? What did not work? What would you do differently today if it happened?

3. Distribute Exercise 51.3. When participants have completed the exercise, ask for feedback. How do they feel as customers?

4. Distribute Exercise 51.4. Here are the answers.

   1. d
   2. c
   3. c
   4. c
   5. d

5. When participants have finished, ask them to find a partner and write an angry statement from one of their customers, and then write a mirroring response. When they have finished, ask them to share their statements and responses with the rest of the group. (Write the responses on a flip chart.)

6. Distribute Exercise 51.5. Ask participants to complete this as individuals.

7. Provide a brief summary and answer any questions before wrapping up.

# When a customer is venting, do not...

■ Get angry yourself.

■ Tell the customer to calm down.

■ Defend yourself.

■ Interrupt.

■ Fail to acknowledge the customer's feelings.

# When a customer is venting,
# Do...

■ Listen actively.

■ Allow the rage to burn out.

■ Visualize the customer cooling down.

■ Breathe calmly.

■ Acknowledge the customer's feelings.

# EXERCISE 51.3: HOW DO I LIKE TO BE TREATED?

Here are ten customer statements. Fill in the word that best describes how you feel in each situation.

1. When there is no follow-through, I feel_____

2. When my name is used, I feel _____

3. When phone calls are returned promptly, I feel _____

4. When people disagree with me, I feel _____

5. When I am interrupted before I have finished speaking, I feel _____

6. When interest is shown in what I am saying, I feel _____

7. When it's acknowledged that I am in a rush, I feel _____

8. When my complaint is not answered promptly, I feel _____

9. When I am appreciated as a customer, I feel _____

10. When I have to wait while someone finishes paperwork, I feel _____

# EXERCISE 51.4: MIRRORING RESPONSES

As a person dealing with the five customer statements below, decide which are the mirroring responses.

1. "The system you recommended has been nothing but trouble."

   a. That's a pity.

   b. Ah, but it was an off-the-floor model.

   c. The system can be difficult to understand.

   d. I am concerned you experienced difficulties with the new system.

2. "I don't normally complain, but I'm very angry. This product is dangerous."

   a. I'm new here. I don't know anything about this product.

   b. It's a new line. It has some teething problems.

   c. I understand that you would want to tell us about something that you consider is dangerous.

   d. What's the problem?

3. "When I unpacked the dinner service, three of the plates were broken. I didn't have time to bring them back and I had important guests that evening. I'm really angry they weren't properly packaged."

   a. They need better training in the packaging department.

   b. We can exchange them now.

   c. How frustrating for you to have important guests and not have all the pieces you wanted. I am sorry.

   d. Was the dinner a success anyway?

4. "This furnace was supposed to be quiet. It keeps us awake all night, and I haven't had a decent night's sleep since it was installed."

   a. I'm surprised they said it would be quiet.

   b. What they say and what it does are two different things.

   c. I'm concerned the furnace is not as quiet as you expected and that it is keeping you awake.

   d. I'll look into it.

5. "When we bought the car you said it would be completely serviced and like a brand new car. This morning it wouldn't start, I was late for my appointment, and I'm really angry."

   a. What a waste of time for you.

   b. Were you able to make another appointment?

   c. Sometimes things go wrong.

   d. I can understand your being angry. You expected the car to be like new and it wouldn't start.

# EXERCISE 51.5: SUPER SERVICE ACTION PLAN

The actions I will take as a result of this activity are:

1.  _____
    _____
    _____
    _____

2.  _____
    _____
    _____
    _____

3.  _____
    _____
    _____
    _____

4.  _____
    _____
    _____
    _____

5.  _____
    _____
    _____

6.  _____
    _____
    _____

I will review this action plan on: _____     _____
                                         (date)                        (signed)

## Background and Purpose

Sometimes when we communicate we build barriers that stop the information from getting through. The purpose of this activity is to find ways to overcome those barriers.

## Objectives

By the end of this activity, participants will be able to:

- Recognize barriers and overcome them.

## Time

Approximately 20 minutes

## Materials Required

There are no materials required for this activity.

## Mini Lecture

Barriers that stop communication include judgments, prejudices, noise, and personal worries. One of the ways to overcome those barriers is to learn how to focus.

Focusing means bringing your whole attention to the person. It means blocking out surrounding noise and your own thoughts and listening actively.

## Steps to Follow

Ask everyone to find a partner (preferably someone they do not know very well). Give them 2 minutes to introduce themselves to each other tell them as much as you can about yourself. Explain that you will tell them when the 2 minutes are up. (Remind them to focus and to actively listen to each other.)

Now ask them to stay with their partners and find two other partner teams

## Activity 52
# Ways to Overcome Barriers

Incorporate the customer's ideas into your solution.

(six people in all). Each person now has 1 minute to introduce his or her partner to the rest of the group.

## Discussion Points

1. How did it feel to listen actively?

2. What were some of the barriers that you had to overcome?

3. How difficult was the exercise?

4. What are some of the things that you will change in order to overcome barriers?

5. How can you use this exercise in your job?

## Background and Purpose

Unhappy customers can become very, very angry. They can use foul language, scream, shout, rant, and rave. Knowing how to deal with an angry customer is very important. The purpose of this activity is to provide tools for customer service providers to use in this situation.

## Objectives

By the end of this activity, participants will be able to:

- Use effective tools to handle an irate customer.

## Time

Approximately 2 hours

## Materials Required

1. Overhead 53.1
2. Flip chart and marker
3. Exercise 53.2

## Mini Lecture

Sometime a customer is irate the minute he or she calls or walks through the door. At other times a customer may go from unhappy to irate during the transaction. Ask the group, "What would cause an unhappy customer to become irate?" Write down their answers on the flip chart.

Possible answers include:

a. The customer is not getting what he or she wants.

b. You are unable to provide what the customer wants.

c. The customer's request is unreasonable.

Ask the group for suggestions on how to overcome these problems.

# Activity 53
# The Irate Customer

It doesn't matter whether customers are right or wrong.
They need to air their complaints.

Possible answers include:

a. Search for alternative solutions.

b. Provide an example of a customer in a similar situation and present that solution.

c. Use empathy and active listening skills.

## Steps to Follow

1. Show Overhead 53.1. Explain that it is not your job to take abuse from irate customers. Here are some ways to defuse an irate customer. Ask the group if they have had any experience of using these techniques.

2. Divide participants into teams of 3. Instruct one person to role play a customer with a typical complaint. The second member is to act as the person who deals with the complaint. The third person acts as observer to give feedback after the role play. Repeat this exercise three times, changing roles so that each team member plays each part. Allow 5 minutes for each role play and 5 minutes for feedback.

3. Distribute Exercise 53.2 and ask participants to complete it individually.

4. Provide a brief summary and answer any questions before wrapping up.

# Ways to Defuse an Irate Customer

- **Visualization**—See the customer as a newborn baby screaming for attention. You are the only person who can calm the customer.

- **Gentle Reminder**—Say: "Is there something I have done personally to upset you? I would like to help you. Please give me a chance."

- **Transfer**—Sometimes the customer is too wild for one person to handle. Say: "I think my manager may be able to help you."

- **Call Security**—If the customer seems about to physically turn on you, say, "I'm sorry, but we need to find a way to work together. I think security will help."

# EXERCISE 53.2: SUPER SERVICE ACTION PLAN

The actions I will take as a result of this activity are:

1. _____

_____

_____

_____

2. _____

_____

_____

_____

3. _____

_____

_____

_____

4. _____

_____

_____

_____

5. _____

_____

_____

_____

6. _____

_____

_____

I will review this action plan on: _____     _____
(date)                                           (signed)

## Activity 54
# Selling Skills

One of the key components of selling is having great energy.

## Background and Purpose

People who provide customer service have a huge potential to help sell their products or services. Often, however, people in this role do not consider themselves salespeople.

The purpose of this activity is to provide an understanding of participants' role in selling, when it is appropriate to sell, and how to do it. The sales technique used in this activity is a questioning technique that is simple and easy to use.

## Objectives

By the end of this activity, participants will be able to:

1. Use a questioning technique as a selling skill.

2. Identify opening, probing, extending, and net gain questions.

## Time

Approximately 3 hours

## Materials Required

1. Overheads 54.1 and 54.2

2. Handout 54.3

3. Exercise 54.4

## Mini Lecture

You may not be aware of it, but you are always selling yourself, your services, or your company. If you think about it, the whole world is a gigantic sales machine. Selling is not just confined to sales and marketing; selling involves every walk of life, including politics, health care, schools, construction, space projects, and so on.

Selling is the ability to get commitment from people. It is getting the customer to say "yes" to something—in our case, to say "yes" to a product or service. As customer service providers, you can have a great impact on the customer's decision to purchase from us again, to upgrade, or to try a different product range.

Ask the group if they can think of any situation when they could be selling.

Possible answers include:

The customer's current product or service does not fit the customer's needs.

An additional part, process, or program is needed to make it function better.

The product is out of date.

An upgrade will enhance the product.

The customer has outgrown the product.

A competitive system they own is incompatible with yours.

## Steps to Follow

1. Show Overhead 54.1. Explain that one of the best sales techniques is called OPEN. It is an acronym for a series of questions that enable you to identify the customer's needs. This technique can be learned easily and can be used in any situation, even at home or with friends.

2. Show Overhead 54.2. Explain that these are examples of OPEN questions.

3. Distribute Handout 54.3. When participants have read it, explain that there is a sequence to asking OPEN questions. Although the sequence may not run exactly in this order, normally Opening questions need to be asked early in the sale, while Net Gain questions need to be asked later in the sale. Opening questions need to be uncovering areas that have a direct impact on your product or service. It does not make sense to ask about the customer's car if your product has no relationship to cars.

   It does not make sense to ask a Probing Question in an area where your product or service provides no solution. A Probing Question needs to examine areas where your customer is experiencing problems and where you can provide a solution.

   Net Gain questions help customers understand what they will gain by accepting your solution. Do not ask these questions if the customer is already saying "yes."

4. Divide participants into teams of 3. Instruct one person to role play a typical customer. The second member is to act as the service provider. The third person acts as observer to give feedback after the role play. Tell the observers that they should jot down every time service providers use an Opening, Probing, Extending, or Net Gain question. Repeat this exercise three times, changing roles so that each team member plays each part. Allow 5 minutes for each role play and 5 minutes for feedback.

   After everyone has played each role, answer any questions and lead a group discussion.

**Discussion topics:**

How did it feel playing the different roles?

Do you see how selling fits in with customer service?

Can you see how the OPEN questioning technique can help in other areas of your life?

5. Distribute Exercise 54.4 and ask participants to complete it individually. If you have time, ask for feedback or ideas.

6. Provide a brief summary and answer any questions before wrapping up.

# OPEN Selling Skills

**O—Opening questions:** Start the sale by understanding the background.

**P—Probing questions:** Reveal problems, difficulties, or dissatisfaction.

**E—Extending questions:** Expand the discussion into other areas.

**N—Net gain questions:** Develop solutions that address needs.

# Examples of OPEN Questions

**O—Opening Question:** "How do you organize your workspace?"

**P—Probing Question:** "What kind of quality issues do you experience?"

**E—Extending Question:** "What effect does this situation have on your delivery system?"

**N—Net Gain Question:** "If you saved 10 cents a plate, how much would that mean in total savings?"

# HANDOUT 54.3

## Opening Questions

*Safe to Use:* With new customers, early in the conversation, or when the customer's situation has changed.

*Hazardous to Use:* Late in the conversation, in sensitive areas, or when you might sound like an interrogator if you ask too many.

## Probing Questions

*Safe to Use:* Early in the conversation, in areas where your product or service can provide solutions, or in areas that are significant to your customer.

*Hazardous to Use:* In sensitive areas such as organizational politics or when the customer has a high personal or emotional involvement, or when your product or service does not provide a solution.

## Extending Questions

*Safe to Use:* When you know the problem can expand into other areas or you can uncover an even greater need; when you can give the customer an additional reason to buy.

*Hazardous to Use:* Too early in the conversation or in areas you cannot address.

## Net Gain Questions

*Safe to Use:* When the answer leads to a payoff in other areas or when the solution must be justified by the customer.

*Hazardous to Use:* Too early in the conversation.

# EXERCISE 54.4: SUPER SERVICE ACTION PLAN

The actions I will take as a result of this activity are:

1. _____
   _____
   _____
   _____

2. _____
   _____
   _____
   _____

3. _____
   _____
   _____
   _____

4. _____
   _____
   _____
   _____

5. _____
   _____
   _____

6. _____
   _____
   _____

I will review this action plan on: _____     _____
                                        (date)                                  (signed)

## Background and Purpose

One of the key components of selling is to have great energy. Developing energy is something that can be learned.

The purpose of this activity is to show participants that their energy level affects every person around them.

## Objectives

By the end of this activity, participants will be able to:

1. Determine how energy affects those around them.

2. Determine what kind of energy makes them feel great.

3. Develop great energy.

## Time

Approximately 1 hour

## Materials Required

1. Overheads 55.1, 55.2, and 55.3

2. Exercises 55.4 and 55.7

3. Role Play Scenarios 55.5

4. Observer's Checklist 55.6

## Mini Lecture

The energy of selling really involves selling yourself. We all have energy. It is what makes us get up in the morning and carries us through the day. We all have different levels of energy. Some of us think and move slowly, others think and move quickly. This activity is not about changing that; it is about understanding our energy and how it affects ourselves and others.

When people act in a positive, cheerful manner, other people usually respond accordingly. Others often start to mirror an enthusiastic demeanor. We all have days when we feel lethargic and

## Activity 55
# Energy for Selling

You can foresee stress.
You can foresee burnout.
You can plan how to handle them.

less lively than on other days; but if you act as though you are energetic and positive, you'll start to feel that way. You can fool people into believing that you feel great, and pretty soon, you will feel great.

## Steps to Follow

1. Show Overhead 55.1. Explain that we all make a choice about the energy that we want to give off to others. It does take an effort, but the more we decide to be a person with great energy, the more it will happen.

2. Show Overhead 55.2. Explain that having energy for selling means being in control of your energy. You are in charge of your energy when you sell. It is your decision whether you want to feel rejected or not.

   **Class Demonstration**

   Hold a pen or pencil and tell the participants to reject you when you ask them to purchase your pen. In other words, tell them that you are going to ask them to purchase your pen, and they are to say "No!" Keep asking different people if they will purchase your pen. They will say no, and you will continue to try to sell it to them. Really try to sell it!

   Continue to keep your energy upbeat. Do not take the rejections to heart. Demonstrate that in real life, if you wanted to sell the pen, you would keep going until you found someone who would say "yes," and that you cannot be rejected unless you decide to be rejected.

3. Show Overhead 55.3. Explain that having great energy does not mean being overbearing or aggressive. It also does not mean being submissive or overly self-critical. Having great energy is about being assertive. That means treating people with respect and treating yourself with respect. You give people a chance to rectify mistakes and to be heard. You do not blame others, but if you are at fault, you do own up and accept responsibility.

4. Distribute Exercise 55.4 and ask participants to complete it individually. Explain that this exercise allows them to see where they are in terms of their own energy and behavior.

   When they have completed the exercise, ask the following questions:

   a. What sort of energy are you exhibiting if you believe someone else's rights are more important than your own? If you believe your rights are more important than anyone else's? If you believe everyone has equal rights?

   b. Have you ever been in a situation in which someone has stared you down? Talked over you? How did it feel?

   c. Think of a person who listens to you and allows you to get your point across. How does that feel?

5. Hand out Role Play Scenarios 55.5 together with Observer's Checklist 55.6. Divide the group into teams of 4. Allow 2 to 3 minutes per role play, 2 to 3 minutes for observer feedback, and 2 to 3 minutes for your

feedback. After each role play, provide the relevant points. Call out the times to ensure every person rotates through each role. Allow 30 to 40 minutes to complete this activity.

Highlight these relevant points:

*Role Play One:* We often take complaints personally and defend ourselves. Instead, say, "I'm sorry to hear that. I understand why you are concerned. If I may, I'll make a note of the details and I can check on what went wrong and how to resolve the situation."

*Role Play Two:* The service provider needed help, but often we are either too hard or too soft with people. A good approach is to say, "Judging by the customer reaction, you came across as abrupt and unsympathetic. I know it's difficult with the pressures we all face, but customers judge us by their terms, not ours. I wanted to have a chat with you to see if there is a problem."

*Role Play Three:* Allocating blame to another department only confirms the customer's negative opinion of the company. Instead, say, "I'm sorry, but it isn't ready yet. It's our fault; we made a mistake. It will be another 15 minutes. Can I get you a cup of coffee while you wait, or should we drop it off at your home tonight? Which do you prefer?"

*Role Play Four:* If we take a hard line, people will dig their heels in. Say instead, "In the past few weeks I have noticed that your time frames have lengthened. This has impacted my projects and we have failed to get back to customers on time. Is there a problem?"

6. Hand out Exercise 55.7 and ask everyone to complete it individually.

7. Provide a brief summary and answer any questions before wrapping up.

# Great Energy

1. Be enthusiastic and gracious.

2. Act in a positive and cheerful manner.

3. Make the first impression good and memorable.

4. Create rapport and a good relationship with others.

# Energy for Selling

1. **Persistence:** *"I'm here to help you, and sooner or later you are going to feel helped."*

2. **Focus:** *"I know what I want, and I will keep directing you back to my goal."*

3. **Assertiveness:** *"I know how much our product has helped others; we just want the opportunity to discuss your needs."*

4. **Self-Motivation:** *"I don't take rejection personally; I move on to the next person."*

# Categories of Energy

1. **Aggressive**—winning even at the expense of other people, ignoring their rights, or being hostile

2. **Submissive**—avoiding conflict even at your own expense, ignoring your own rights, or being self-critical

3. **Assertive**—standing up for your own rights, acknowledging the rights of others, and looking for win–win solutions

## EXERCISE 55.4

PARTICIPANT'S
HANDOUT

We can categorize people's energy as aggressive, submissive, or assertive. Circle the behavior that most closely matches your own energy pattern.

| *Aggressive* | *Submissive* | *Assertive* |
|---|---|---|
| Always uses "I" | Hardly ever uses "I" | Uses "I" when necessary |
| Hard-hitting, to-the-point | Hesitant and rambling | To-the-point in a neutral way |
| Opinions are expressed as true facts | Follows opinions of others | Draws a line between facts and opinions |
| Uses sarcasm and personal criticism | Says "sorry" a lot and seeks permission | Straightforward expression, requests explanations |
| Blames others | Very self-critical | Seeks solutions |
| Voice is loud and fast, can be cold and sharp | Voice is soft, dull, flat, slow, and hesitant | Firm, clear, and understandable voice; interesting and holds attention |
| Holds eye contact too long | Looks down with little or no eye contact | Eye contact is steady and comfortable |
| Points finger or thumps table | Hand-washing and fidgeting | Expressive, open hands |
| Invades personal space, domineering | Shrinks away from people | Stands upright, shows concern and attention as appropriate |

334

# ROLE PLAY SCENARIOS 55.5

Here are four role plays. One group member will play the employee and another the customer, while the other members act as observers and provide feedback to the person playing the role of Employee, Manager, or Team Leader. Start with role play one, then rotate as directed by your facilitator. You will all play each role at least once.

## Role Play One

*Employee:* You are a new employee with the company. You have just returned from a break. You are standing behind the counter when the customer approaches.

*Customer:* You are very annoyed. You bought an item last week for a special occasion or presentation. When you got it home or to the office, it was completely the wrong item. Your plan was totally destroyed.

## Role Play Two

*Manager:* You overheard an employee talking to a customer in an unsympathetic and abrupt manner. It is the third time this week you have noticed it. You have asked the employee to come to your office to talk about it.

*Service Provider:* Normally you can handle customer problems, even though you have a lot going on in your personal life. Today it got to you, and you just don't want to listen to any more problems.

## Role Play Three

*Employee:* Your customer has come to pick up the item that was ordered. It will not be ready for another 15 minutes. Due to a departmental error, a particular feature that the customer wanted did not get installed on time.

*Customer:* You have come to pick up the item you ordered last week. You have another appointment in 15 minutes.

## Role Play Four

*Team Leader:* You are leading a project that has a direct impact on customers. One person on the team has consistently failed to do the job on time. This has impacted your schedule so that you have been late getting back to customers. You have decided to speak to the team member about it.

*Team Member:* Along with everything else on your plate, a senior VP learned about your special interest or hobby and asked you to put together some very detailed information on it. Although it has taken more time than you thought, you have almost finished it.

# OBSERVER'S CHECKLIST 55.6

This checklist will help you give feedback. Use it as a guide and write your observer notes on a separate sheet of paper. When you get feedback, summarize the comments below.

| | |
|---|---|
| **Did you take responsibility for the problem?** | |
| Were you empathetic? | |
| Were you solution-oriented? | |
| What aggressive tendencies did you exhibit? | |
| What submissive tendencies did you exhibit? | |
| What assertive tendencies did you exhibit? | |
| What would you do differently? | |

# EXERCISE 55.7: SUPER SERVICE ACTION PLAN

The actions I will take as a result of this activity are:

1. _____

   _____

   _____

   _____

2. _____

   _____

   _____

   _____

3. _____

   _____

   _____

4. _____

   _____

   _____

5. _____

   _____

   _____

6. _____

   _____

   _____

I will review this action plan on: _____      _____
                                        (date)                              (signed)

## Background and Purpose

Even though many people use E-mail today, the telephone is still a powerful tool. Customers form opinions very quickly on the telephone, and it is easy to end up with a dissatisfied customer. Because of this, professional telephone behavior is very important and requires up-to-date guidelines.

The purpose of this activity is to provide guidelines and tips for professional telephone behavior.

## Objectives

By the end of this activity, participants will be able to:

1. Understand guidelines for professional telephone behavior.

2. Measure their own behavior against those guidelines.

3. Develop an action plan for improvement.

## Time

Approximately 1 hour and 45 minutes

## Materials Required

1. Flip chart and marker

2. Overheads 56.1 and 56.2

3. Exercises 56.3 and 56.4

## Mini Lecture

Telephones play an important role in any organization. Customers quickly determine if the person who answers the phone is willing and able to help them or not, just by listening to the tone of voice. Telephones can be the most wonderful tools for communicating and also the most frustrating.

Ask the following question: "How many times a week do you talk to customers on the telephone?" Record the total

## Activity 56

# The Telephone

In the business world, the phone is like a screwdriver. It can open things and close things, and it can also screw things up.

sum on the flip chart and explain that this is the number of times it is possible to have a dissatisfied customer.

If you do not use professional telephone skills, you will not only have dissatisfied customers, you may also lose customers.

## Steps to Follow

1. Ask the group to brainstorm the number of ways it is possible for a telephone conversation to go wrong. Record the answers on the flip chart.

   **Possible answers include:**

   Being left on hold

   Put through to an extension that just rings and rings

   Not getting a reply fast enough

   Being connected to the wrong extension

   Not knowing who you are talking with or what department

   Being called at an inconvenient time

   Not knowing what will happen next after the call has ended

2. Divide the group into teams of 4 to 5. Ask them to write down the pitfalls and benefits of telephone communication.

   **Possible answers include:**

   *Pitfalls*

   No body language to aid communication

   Intrusion onto people's time

   Being distracted and unable to listen carefully

   Unable to communicate complicated information

   *Benefits*

   Easier and quicker way to contact people

   People have less to judge a person by

   Positions of authority are less obvious

3. Show Overhead 56.1. Explain the importance of returning calls immediately. People judge your level of responsibility and ability to organize by whether you return calls or not. Ask the participants to think of people who do not return calls. Also point out the importance of keeping messages short. Explain that it is important to tell the person what response you need: a return call, confirmation of a date, a telephone number.

4. Show Overhead 56.2. Explain that everyone's voice sounds different. It reflects your personality and attitude. If you are angry, you will sound angry. Voices

can be clear, squeaky, difficult to decipher, monotonous, low-pitched, or high-pitched. Choose words that can easily be understood; be caring and confident. Speak at a rate that is not too fast or too slow. Adjust the volume of your voice to match the customer's volume, *unless the customer is shouting!*

5. Distribute Exercise 56.3. Ask the participants to read through the exercise and look for factors that assisted the communication process and factors that hindered it. Ask them for feedback and debrief using these notes:

**Factors that hindered include:**

Detached manner of the operator (despite words used)

No chance to describe the problem and get the correct connection

The voice was impersonal; no introduction, empathy, or interest

Mary, the customer, never asked if anyone else could help

The message left for John gave no information

**Factors that assisted include:**

Enthusiastic operator determines the problem

Communicates delays promptly

Introductions are made

Problems are summarized, saving the customer from repeating them

Standard form records details

Action is confirmed

When they are finished, ask them to brainstorm (as a group) a set of guidelines that, if followed, would lead to professional telephone behavior. Write down the answers on the flip chart. When they have finished, ask them to number the guidelines in order of importance.

Ask them to write the list down and refer to it often.

6. Distribute Exercise 56.4. Ask participants to complete it as individuals.

7. Provide a brief summary and answer any questions before wrapping up.

# Return Calls Immediately.

# Keep Messages Short.

# Include the Response You Need.

- Rate of Speech

- Volume

- Tone

- Diction

# EXERCISE 56.3

Read the two scenarios and make notes on what hindered the communication process and what assisted the process.

## Scenario One

Mary Hall manages an office that relies fully on its large computer network system. Six weeks ago she received an incorrect invoice for computer services. She wrote to the service company, and three weeks later received a letter apologizing for the error and stating that her account would be credited. The invoice she received today does not show the credit. She is angry and telephones the company.

"Thank you for calling *Compute Future*, Bill speaking. How may I help you?" the voice sings out in a detached and efficient manner.

"Finance, please," says Mary abruptly.

"Putting you thr…" Bill makes the connection before he finishes the sentence. Mary hears the phone ring ten times before the extension is finally answered.

"Hello," says a voice.

"Is this the finance department?" asks Mary.

"Yes," answers the voice.

"I'd like to speak to the manager, please," states Mary in a direct voice.

"He's not here," says the voice.

"Great!" says Mary, obviously frustrated. "Tell him to call me as soon as he gets back or I'm writing to your Chief Executive, canceling my contract. I hope that's clear."

"Yes, I'll put the message on his desk now," says the voice.

"Be sure you do that." Mary bangs the phone down.

"The voice" leaves the following message on the finance manager's desk: **"John, please call Mary Hall."**

## Scenario Two

A similar error was made with Bill Hunt's company. He calls the service company to find out about the invoice.

"Good morning, *Compute Present*," answers the operator in a pleasant voice.

"Finance department, please," says Bill in an abrupt and annoyed voice.

"May I ask what it's in connection with, please?" asks the operator.

"A wrong invoice," says Bill, still annoyed.

"I'll put you through to the section that handles invoices. May I ask who's calling?"

"Bill Hunt."

"Putting you through." Within a second the operator comes back on the line. "The extension is busy, Mr. Hunt. I'll try another."

A few seconds later, a man's voice comes through.

"Hello, Mr. Hunt. I'm Jane Sanders. I understand you have an incorrect invoice."

"Yes. I want to speak to your manager," demands Bill.

"He's out sick today and won't be in until tomorrow. I work in the invoice section. May I help, please?"

Moments later, Jane uses a standard form to record Mr. Hunt's company name, address, account number, and the details of the incorrect invoice. "Mr. Hunt, I have enough information to begin checking and I'm going to do that right away. I'll get back to you with an answer by this afternoon. Can I reach you all day at the number you gave me?"

"Yes, that's right. Thank you, Jane, you've been very helpful."

# EXERCISE 56.4: SUPER SERVICE ACTION PLAN

The actions I will take as a result of this activity are:

1. _____
   _____
   _____
   _____

2. _____
   _____
   _____
   _____

3. _____
   _____
   _____

4. _____
   _____
   _____
   _____

5. _____
   _____
   _____

6. _____
   _____
   _____

I will review this action plan on: _____  _____
                                             (date)                               (signed)

# Activity 57
# How to Transfer a Call

## Background and Purpose

Transferring a call seems like a very easy thing to do, and it is, as long as a few very simple rules are followed.

The purpose of this activity is to demonstrate the correct procedure and identify the rules.

## Objectives

By the end of this activity, participants will be able to:

1. Understand the importance of transferring a call correctly.

2. Identify the correct procedure.

## Time

Approximately 45 minutes

## Materials Required

1. Overhead 57.1

2. Flip chart and marker

3. Exercise 57.2

## Mini Lecture

How many of you have had bad experiences being transferred by phone? (Feedback should highlight: transfers to wrong department or person, being cut off, left holding for too long, repeating the problem again and again.)

How does it make you feel if the transfer goes through smoothly, and what makes it go smoothly? (Feedback should highlight: not left on hold, not cut off, problem is identified, transferred to correct department.)

Is transferring calls part of your job?

Explain that most of us have to transfer calls at some time or another. Often, if we think the call is personal or does not relate to our job or position, we don't treat the caller with professional courtesy. The problem is that it is too easy to be discourteous on the telephone—especially if we are transferring a call that does not involve someone we know.

## Steps to Follow

1. Show Overhead 57.1. Explain that the guidelines for transferring a call follow a useful acronym that helps us to remember how to do it effectively. Take some time to discuss each of the ideas. Be aware that some of these steps may not fit every participant's needs. For example, they may not have the ability or need to add on calls or stay on the line. Match the steps to the needs of the group. Identify any steps that do not fit and highlight the steps that do. Write the new steps on a flip chart.

   **Take Time**—"Linda in accounts will be able to answer your question; this is her area of expertise."

   **Request Permission**—"May I put you on hold for a moment while I put you through to the right person?"

   **Add on Calls**—"I'll stay on the line until Linda joins our call."

   **Never Hold Too Long**—Being on hold for a long time is very frustrating.

   **Stay on the Line**—If this is a feature of your telephone system, stay on the line until the right person is found. "Thank you for holding. This is Linda from accounts, Mr. Bachman. I've explained your problem to her. Linda, this is Mr. Bachman."

   **Focus on Issues**—"Is there anything else I can help you with today?"

   **Empathize**—"I know how frustrating this must have been for you. I hope the problem has been resolved to your satisfaction."

   **Remember Your Input**—"I'm very pleased to be of service. Please call again if there is anything else we can help you with."

2. Group participants into pairs. Ask each pair to transfer a typical call. One acts as a service provider and one as a customer. Allow 2 to 3 minutes and then ask them to switch roles. Ask for feedback. What worked? What did not work? What will they do differently in the future?

3. Distribute Exercise 57.2 and ask participants to complete it individually.

4. Provide a brief summary and answer any questions before wrapping up.

# How to Transfer a Call

T—Take time to communicate.

R—Request permission.

A—Add on calls while remaining on the line.

N—Never put people on hold longer than 2 minutes.

S—Stay on the line until the problem is resolved.

F—Focus on solving the customer's issues.

E—Empathize with your customers.

R—Remember, you make the difference.

# EXERCISE 57.2: SUPER SERVICE ACTION PLAN

The actions I will take as a result of this activity are:

1. _____

_____

_____

_____

2. _____

_____

_____

_____

3. _____

_____

_____

4. _____

_____

_____

5. _____

_____

_____

6. _____

_____

_____

I will review this action plan on: _____ _____
(date)                                          (signed)

## Background and Purpose

Everyone has to take and leave messages over the telephone at some time or another. It seems like a very simple thing to do, and it is, so long as a few simple rules and guidelines are followed.

The purpose of this activity is to highlight the rules.

## Objective

By the end of this activity, participants will be able to:

- Understand the rules for taking and leaving an accurate message.

## Time

Approximately 20 minutes

## Materials Required

1. Overheads 58.1 and 58.2

2. Exercise 58.3

## Mini Lecture

Taking a message is very simple. It can also create many problems if it is not done correctly. This is a very simple activity to outline a few rules about taking and leaving messages.

## Steps to Follow

1. Show Overhead 58.1. Explain that taking a message must be done when the person to whom the caller wishes to speak is unavailable.

   Ask the group for experiences with taking messages. If possible, provide an example of what happens when messages are not taken accurately. For example, a person is responding to an interview call. The message gets lost and the person (a potential internal customer) loses the opportunity of getting the job. Or a

---

## Activity 58
# How to Take an Accurate Message

Imagining what it is like to be your customer is a powerful customer service technique.

customer has called once already and the messages are not being picked up because they are posted in the wrong location.

2. Show Overhead 58.2. Explain that it is your responsibility to leave an accurate message. For this, you must give the urgency of the message and the action required. For example, if a house deed must be signed before close of business that day, the message must incorporate those details. It would be important to find out when the person collects messages. Do you need to call another number? Does the person pick up E-mail messages sooner than phone messages?

Ask the group for experiences with leaving messages. Use feedback to highlight key points.

3. Distribute Exercise 58.3 and ask participants to complete it individually.

4. Provide a brief summary and answer any questions before wrapping up.

## Taking an Accurate Message

1.  Time

2.  Date

3.  Caller's name, company, job title

4.  Telephone number and extension

5.  Message in detail

6.  Best time to return call

7.  Sign the message

8.  Place message in clear view

9.  Note any action needed

10. Urgency

# Leaving an Accurate Message

1. Name, company, job title

2. Telephone number and extension

3. Message in detail

4. Action Required

5. Urgency

6. Repeat for accuracy

7. Availability (for receiving return call)

# EXERCISE 58.3: SUPER SERVICE ACTION PLAN

The actions I will take as a result of this activity are:

1.  _____
    _____
    _____
    _____

2.  _____
    _____
    _____
    _____

3.  _____
    _____
    _____

4.  _____
    _____
    _____
    _____

5.  _____
    _____
    _____

6.  _____
    _____
    _____

I will review this action plan on: _____     _____
                                             (date)                                    (signed)

## Activity 59

# Using the Phone with a Computer

## Background and Purpose

Most organizations are tied into computer systems. Many customer service providers sit with a phone terminal in one ear, looking at a computer screen. The problem is that the customer becomes a nonperson—just a bunch of numbers on a screen.

The purpose of this activity is to provide customer service providers with a set of tools to ensure that they treat the customer as a customer.

## Objectives

By the end of this activity, participants will be able to:

1. Understand the pitfalls of treating the customer as a "number."

2. Follow key steps in the process of using the phone with a computer.

## Time

Approximately 45 minutes

## Materials Required

1. Overheads 59.1 and 59.2

2. Exercise 59.3

## Mini Lecture

A large marine company has a customer service department that deals with agents who purchase their equipment. The service providers need the agents' numbers to access all their information on-screen. The service providers are so focused on getting the agents' numbers that the first words out of their mouths are, "What's your number?" If an angry customer calls, he or she is still greeted with, "What's your number?"

When this happens, it is like being discounted. A better way to handle the situation would be to listen to at least one or two sentences of the caller's problem and, when you have some understanding of the issues, say, "I understand your problem. May I have your agent number so I can help you by viewing all your information on my screen?"

The management of the marine company believed that if they got the call rate as high as possible, they would be providing good customer care. In reality, all that's happening is that their call rate is high.

## Steps to Follow

1. Show Overhead 59.1. Explain that much of customer service depends on your attitude. As a customer service provider, you are also selling your service, so it is important to keep these concepts in mind.

2. Show Overhead 59.2. Explain that these guidelines can be customized to fit their needs, but basically, these elements need to be included in any customer service call via telephone. The verbal handshake means identifying who you are and who you represent. If you are making a call, ask if it is convenient to talk; if you are receiving a call, ask how you can help.

   Signing off properly means stating what will happen next and thanking the other person for his or her time.

   Remember that all telephone users have rights. Both you and other people have a right to:

   Know who is on the other end of the call.

   Say if it is inconvenient to talk at that time.

   Express needs and be heard.

   Ask questions to clarify and check details.

   Understand what the other person will do after the call and what is expected of you.

3. Divide the participants into groups of 3 or 4. Ask each group to make a list of the most common pitfalls of using the telephone in their jobs. Ask them to exchange their completed lists with another group. Now ask them to find solutions to the pitfalls listed by the other group.

   Begin a group discussion by asking:

   Were the pitfalls much the same?

   What were the solutions?

4. Distribute Exercise 59.3 and ask participants to complete it as individuals.

5. Provide a brief summary and answer any questions before wrapping up.

# Telephone Attitude

1. Be enthusiastic and positive.

2. Want to do best for the customer.

3. Leave a great last impression.

4. Remember that rejection is not personal.

5. Believe in your product or service.

# Telephone Guidelines

- Answer telephone within three rings.

- Don't leave callers hanging on.

- Give a verbal handshake.

- Determine what information you need.

- Control call by asking appropriate questions.

- Read important information back to clarify.

- Sign off properly.

# EXERCISE 59.3: SUPER SERVICE ACTION PLAN

The actions I will take as a result of this activity are:

1. _____
   _____
   _____
   _____

2. _____
   _____
   _____
   _____

3. _____
   _____
   _____

4. _____
   _____
   _____

5. _____
   _____
   _____

6. _____
   _____
   _____

I will review this action plan on: _____   _____
                                       (date)                                 (signed)

## Background and Purpose

Everyone experiences stress and burnout at some time or another. The important thing is to know how to deal with it.

The purpose of this activity is to help participants understand that stress is normal and to provide tools for handling it.

## Objectives

By the end of this activity, participants will be able to:

1. Understand the role that stress plays.

2. Use tools for handling day-to-day stress.

## Time

Approximately 45 minutes

## Materials Required

1. Overheads 60.1 and 60.2

2. Exercises 60.3 and 60.4

## Mini Lecture

Imagine a high-wire performer. Halfway through the act, the wire gets so stressed that it snaps and the performer falls. Imagine a forest. A blazing fire spreads out of control and burns every tree (including the mature redwoods and young saplings). The high-wire performer wasn't stressed, and the forest didn't start the fire; however, both suffered as a result of coming into contact with stress and burnout.

You are neither a high-wire performer nor a tree. However, you do have customers, and customers are potential initiators of stress. Even though they are not you, they can affect you, so that you feel stressed and burned out. This happens when you ignore the warning signals.

## Activity 60

# How to Avoid Stress and Burnout

A wise person once said, "God always sends pebbles before the rocks." The best way to avoid stress and burnout is to take notice of the pebbles. Let's say you are having a so-so day: not good, not bad. An irate customer calls, and you handle it. Your boss is angry, and you handle it. Another angry customer calls, and you handle it. A coworker wants help with a problem that should have been solved by now; and you handle it. You have lunch. The food is terrible and everyone is talking about a TV show you didn't see. You feel isolated. Back on the job, your boss is angry over something that wasn't your fault. Another customer calls with a complaint you don't have the authority to solve. You pass it along to a manager who is annoyed that you didn't handle it. It's nearing the end of your day; your boss asks you to stay late. Finally, you leave work. You feel miserable. You get home and you feel either lonely because no one is around, or confined because too many people are around.

Whatever your scenario, you feel miserable. The same things happen the next day and the next, until you have a chronic situation. You are drowning in an ongoing cycle of stress and burnout. You feel the only way out is to get another job.

You get another job. The problem is, the same things start happening.

## Steps to Follow

1. Show Overhead 60.1. Explain that the first thing to understand about stress is that our reaction to it is always a choice. Even when the worst things happen (and things get in our path), it is our choice how we handle them. Think of Bill Cosby. His son was murdered, but he still does comedy. Bill Clinton was impeached, but he still made decisions as the president. We can feel stressed or sad, but at some point, we make the decision to get on with our lives.

   Ask the group if they know of anyone (or have experienced) making this choice. Ask for feedback on what tools they used.

2. Show Overhead 60.2. Explain that doing research ahead of time and knowing when to expect a stressful situation really does help. Then you can identify solutions: How are things run? What is the culture? You can plan how to bring your solutions into effect by asking yourself, "How can I fit in?" Finally, plan your reward. If you have headed off a potentially stressful situation, do reward yourself.

3. Distribute Exercise 60.3. Ask participants to complete it as individuals. When they have finished, elicit feedback by asking the following questions:

   How much do other people play a part in your stress?

   What are some of the solutions?

   How will you put your solutions into practice?

   What are some of the rewards you plan to give yourself?

4. Distribute Exercise 60.4. Ask participants to complete it as individuals.

5. Provide a brief summary and answer any questions before wrapping up.

## Stress and Burnout

The stressed wire and forest fire had nothing to do with the high-wire performer or the trees. They just happened to be in the path.

An angry customer, boss, or coworker has nothing to do with you. They just happen to be in your path.

## Foresee Stressful Situations

Identify stressful situations ahead of time.

Identify solutions.

Plan how to bring your solutions into effect.

Plan your reward.

**EXERCISE 60.3**

Write one sentence to describe the most stressful situation in your job at this moment:

_____

_____

_____

_____

Write out two solutions that will help relieve this situation:

1. _____

_____

_____

_____

2. _____

_____

_____

Write down your reward. Choose something that you really enjoy and that does not cost a lot of money or take a lot of time.

_____

_____

_____

_____

# EXERCISE 60.4: SUPER SERVICE ACTION PLAN

The actions I will take as a result of this activity are:

1.  _____
    _____
    _____
    _____

2.  _____
    _____
    _____
    _____

3.  _____
    _____
    _____
    _____

4.  _____
    _____
    _____
    _____

5.  _____
    _____
    _____
    _____

6.  _____
    _____
    _____

I will review this action plan on: _____     _____
                                          (date)                                       (signed)

## About the Authors

**Val Gee** is an instructional designer, an ordained priest, and a regular contributor to *Training* magazine.

**Jeff Gee** is a popular motivational speaker and trainer with over 20 years' experience.

Val and Jeff are principals of McNeil & Johnson, which has trained over 250,000 people since 1986. They are the authors of *Super Service*.